FROM PRISON
TO THE
PREMIERSHIP

FROM PRISON
TO THE
PREMIERSHIP

The Amazing True Story of Britain's
Hardest Footballer

JAMIE LAWRENCE

JOHN BLAKE

Published by John Blake Publishing Ltd,
3, Bramber Court, 2 Bramber Road,
London W14 9PB, England

www.blake.co.uk

First published in hardback in 2006

ISBN 1 84454 205 X

British Library Cataloguing-in-Publication Data:

A catalogue record for this book is available from the British Library.

Design by www.envydesign.co.uk

Printed in Great Britain by Creative, Print & Design

1 3 5 7 9 10 8 6 4 2

© Text copyright Jamie Lawrence

Papers used by John Blake Publishing are natural, recyclable products
made from wood grown in sustainable forests. The manufacturing
processes conform to the environmental regulations of the country
of origin.

Every attempt has been made to contact the relevant copyright-holders, but
some were unobtainable. We would be grateful if the appropriate people
could contact us.

To my mum Elfreda, dad Dudley RIP,
sister Valerie, Ray, Nathan, Tiagh, Tamara
and Rowena and all my nephews, nieces and
family too numerous to mention.
I love you all.

ACKNOWLEDGEMENTS

I must give a shout out to my bredrens Gee, Fat Sam, Reds, Paul 'Big Nose' Speller, Simmo and Luton who shared some precious moments, fun times and helped me get through tough times.

Winston Clarke has always been there for me and I respect him both as a friend and father-figure. Thanks Wins. Ron Shillingford who helped put this book together. Anita Smith, who gave me so much of her time at Bradford as if she were my personal secretary, I love you. Geoffrey Richmond, the Bradford chairman. You had your faults but you were always alright with me. Thank you. Jimmy 'Whack' Walker, aka Donnie Brascoe. He should be a black man, because he moves like one! Lesley, even though I haven't seen Tamara for five years, I know you've brought her up right and deserve props for that. Tasha too, you deserve a big-up for the way you're guiding Nathan.

All those people who helped me in my career and never lost faith: Coach Carl Brown, Alistair Airey, Paul Jewell, Martin O'Neill, John Sackett, Dale Young, Eddie Walder and Coach Sebastiao Lazzaroni. Others who deserve props are Emile Heskey, Wayne Titch RIP and Andrew Titch RIP, Mary and Mick Whelan, Rivs, Jacko, Timothy 'Bobsy' Hague, Walshie and the brothers Mark, Scully, Roger, Maurice and Stephen Hills. Ryan, Adrian, Glenroy, Don Goodman, Stuart McCall, Beags, Dean Saunders, Big Stan Collymore, Jakes, Darren Moore, Rammers, Barry 'Beefy' Hayles, Micah Hyde, Warren Hackett, Ryan Kirby, O'Neil Donaldson, Sammy Chung, George Smith, Nicky Law, Ronnie Glavin, Muzzy Izzet, Neil Lennon, Steve Walford, Paul Franklin and John Robertson. Thanks to Pete Rhodes, Andy Cole and Isiah Rankin.

Also a special big up to Andy Myers, Giles, Platts, Nicky, Homer and Mick Lonergan. Jasbo, you should be a stand-up comedian. Finally, big thanks to my publisher John Blake for your faith in this project and Clive Hebard for all your patient editing.

CONTENTS

Introduction   xi

1 Don't Mug Me Off!   1

2 In at the Deep End   7

3 Roadrunner's Too Fast   19

4 Held for Murder   37

5 Get Me Out of Here!   51

6 Spiv Mentality   69

7 Butcher's Best   85

8 Premier Quality   103

9 Revenge on the Backstabber   115

10 Against All Expectations   129

11 Bantams Welcome   141

12 Perk of the Job   159

13 Keeping Wolves at Bay   171

14 On the Reggae Beat   183

15 Crisis Valley   209

16 Survival Instincts   223

17 End of an Era   233

18 Samba Lesson   253

19 Right Side of the Law   263

20 Angry Bee   281

INTRODUCTION

The saying goes that first impressions are always lasting ones. When I first met Jamie Lawrence he had this stupid 'pineapple' hairstyle and a bad boy reputation which meant I didn't take him seriously. He turned out to be a kind and considerate person, a treasure to handle as a manager and always keen to show the right level of discipline. Jamie is one of the nicest players I've had the pleasure to work with. What he's achieved in such a short space of time is incredible. As a teenager he was written off as a footballer, one of life's losers. But his big heart and total commitment to turning his life around has made him a success story that should inspire anyone who has made mistakes in their life and feels despair.

It is never too late to change your life for the better. Jamie is testament to that. Considering where he came from only a few years ago, who would have thought he would establish himself not just as a quality Premiership player but also a Jamaican international with many caps? I am very proud of him and wish him every success in the future. After such a bad start in life things can only get better. Good luck Jamie.

Paul Jewell, former Bradford City manager

Chapter 1

DON'T MUG ME OFF!

Bam! The snooker cue crashed down on my head and broke in two. Luckily, I had seen it coming out of the corner of my eye otherwise the middle would have scored a direct hit and I might not be here today. Thankfully, the Lord blessed me with a very hard head. The pain was terrible, but anger and adrenaline kicked in.

I was about nineteen and fearless. Donovan, the local bad boy, thought he could take me out and save himself a beating. The attack stemmed from a £50 bet he refused to pay – a lot of dough then. Dazed, with claret dripping from my busted forehead and furious, I pulled a ratchet knife out of the back of my pocket and lashed out. It caught him across the neck. He screamed like a banshee. The blood seeped down in a thin, horizontal line. He was lucky it didn't catch the

1

jugular but it caused a bubble-gum scar, which you can still see to this day.

Donovan was two years older than me and a nutter, who loved taking liberties. But he couldn't intimidate me. I used to see him at Battersea Snooker Hall and thinking he could make some easy dough, he challenged me. The bet was £10, but after I won he wanted double or quits. When he lost again, he agreed to play for a bulls-eye (£50), which in those days was like winning the lottery. It was a lot of 'paper' and the culture in our circles was that you always paid up, always. It was a point of honour.

Super-confident, I gave him a twenty-point head start every time. Small for my age and looking younger, he probably thought I was an easy victim. Donovan couldn't believe it when he lost and said he would pay later, but he stopped coming to the snooker hall. Someone told me he was always in the New World Snooker Club in Battersea Rise. So I went there and confronted him: 'Where's my money?' He claimed he didn't have it, but when you play for cash, you're supposed to have it on you. If I didn't have enough and lost, I had plenty of backers in the hall to help, but no one trusted him. So I said, 'When am I going to get it?' But he wouldn't give a precise time. 'You're still mugging me off,' I replied.

So I said we'd better go outside and sort it out. As we walked out, that's when he crashed the cue over my head. Them days everyone carried a knife, more for self-defence and intimidation than anything – if it wasn't a ratchet, it was either a 007 knife or a lock-knife. I was so furious that it would not have bothered me if I'd killed him. Red mist descended. He screamed and took off. I thought Ben Johnson [the Candian athlete] was quick, but Donovan was faster than Johnson on steroids. I chased, but he was so scared he disappeared – lucky for him 'cos I would have done some proper damage.

A few days later I was walking along Lavender Hill, past the police station, pushing a pram with my one-year-old niece in it, when I bumped into Donovan. He still had the bandage round his neck. What a surreal situation! Still fuming, I asked, 'Where's my dough?' Anything could have happened, but he sheepishly peeled off my money and just gave it to me.

* * * * *

This is my world, my experience of growing up in some of the roughest parts of south London, where it pays to be quick-witted, handy with your fists and brave enough to use a tool if you have to. It's been the story of my life, not allowing anyone to take liberties, it's got me into a lot of scrapes, but that is how I am. Even now I sometimes have to bad up some people to get my money. For example, no one likes tales being told about them and this guy from my favourite pub, the Beaufoy Arms in Lavender Hill, Battersea, started spreading a lie that I was sleeping with someone's wife just because he'd seen me talking to her a couple of times in the pub. I confronted him and he admitted being a liar. I banned him from coming in the Beaufoy when I was there. But one day he turned up with his Yardie mates, proper gangsta Jamaicans, and carried on as if he owned the place. I didn't do anything, but the next time I was in there and walked into the toilets, guess who was there? A few digs to the ribs and he was out. No head shots. That would leave bruises. No one likes grasses – he knew he was out of order and I knew he wouldn't go to the police. Two years later he came in, thinking the ban was over. I poured a pint of Guinness over his head. He's never been back...

Another time, my tailor sold me four Gucci bags he promised were not 'moody'. They were almost full price but they fell apart after a few weeks. He was making good money from me, £20 for a £10 cut. But this was business. Expecting a full refund, I was very patient, but after three months he was still stalling. When you play football they think you've got X-amount of money and that you don't care how much you pay. I told him, 'My word is my bond and when I do a deal with someone who's supposed to be my bredren [friend] I don't expect to be mugged off. There's no NatWest cashpoint here – I've got financial responsibilities and kids to feed! You're having my pants down and spanking my arse!'

Because I'm generally easygoing, when I switched on him I felt like a bully, but my bredren said they were surprised I'd let it go this long. Furious, I told one bredren to have a word with him otherwise things were going to get ugly. The money started coming the next day.

Ask anyone who knows me well and they'll tell you I'm an easygoing, very fair and generous guy. But never mug Jamie Lawrence off. It's not in my nature to let people take advantage. From prison to the Premiership, I've got one hell of a story to tell. This is my colourful past – so far.

Chapter 2

IN AT THE DEEP END

Life in the sixties was tough for Caribbean immigrants. No matter how qualified they were, only menial jobs – mainly in factories, hospitals and the transport services – were offered to them. During the post-war years Britain was still rebuilding itself and my parents' generation was invited to help put the 'Great' back in Britain; only for them the streets were paved with more misery than gold.

It was especially hard for Mum (Elfreda) and my step-dad (Dudley). They already had eight kids between them when they met, me being the youngest of the batch. Mum had three children in Jamaica (Beverly, Leonie and Glenroy) and Valerie in London. Dudley's three 'back home' were Ken, Carlton and Sharon. He also had another two, Beverly and Paul, here. In those days it was hard enough for immigrants to survive, but with all those needy kids, they could not afford to waste a single penny.

Valerie, who is four years older than me, is my closest sibling. Twenty years older than me, Beverly was the only one of Mum's Jamaica-born kids to come over. She was four months pregnant with her second child, Ray Grant, when I was born and she had another, Abdul (aka Shola), two years later. Mum was married to Leon when she first came to England and as far as I was concerned, he was biological father to me and Val as he'd always been in the background. The truth would come out years later. Bev's father died in Jamaica when she was a baby. Sadly, Beverly died of kidney and lung failure when I was a toddler and two of her three sons – Ray Grant and Abdul – later came to live with us. Richard, her eldest son, already lived with his dad. Ray and Shola may have been my nephews, but we grew up like brothers and I am still close to Ray today.

I was always good at sports, excelled in all of them. Football, cricket, athletics… every one but swimming. That comes from the time I went to the local baths, aged seven, with Val. We went in the holidays with the carers from the play centre so there was no great supervision. As I had taught myself to swim in the bath I thought it would be just the same in the pool. So I jumped in at the deep end – and dropped to the bottom. Terrified, gulping in the water, my life looked over before it had started. Luckily, Valerie saw me in distress, jumped in and pulled me out. I've been swimming since to try to conquer my mind but never feel comfortable. Water is for fishes.

* * * * *

James Hubert Lawrence came into the world around ten o'clock one sunny Sunday morning, on 8 March 1970 at the South London Hospital for Women on Clapham Common South Side. My little fists were already locked in a boxer's stance and I've been a fighter ever since. I was named after Mum's dad. She is from 'Bombay', the red dirt area of Manchester, Jamaica. Dudley, my step-dad, was from Portland. Valerie remembers the day when Mum went to the hospital to have the baby. She was so pleased to have a little brother and got very excited when she was allowed to hold me. The bond was instant and we've been close ever since.

Mum, Val and me lived in Chestnut Grove, Balham, a private house divided into two separate living quarters. It was shared with the landlady and cost £8 a week, a fortune. Leon was estranged from Mum and lived nearby in Herne Hill, while Dudley lived further south in Brockley. Leon used to try to track Mum down and even after they divorced, he caused trouble with Dudley. He once went to his workplace in New Cross and tried to shake him off a tall ladder before being stopped by onlookers. As far as I was concerned, Dudley was my real dad. He showed he loved Val and I like his own.

But Mum couldn't afford to stay in Balham and so we eventually got a high-rise council flat in Totteridge House, Battersea. Not ideal, but at least it had two bedrooms. We stayed there for about a year before Wandsworth Council moved us to Dunston Road, Battersea, into a three-bed brand new semi-detached house. After the high-rise it was like a palace, with a back and front garden. By now Dudley was living with us, and when we moved in, Ray and Shola came, too. The three boys slept in the biggest bedroom. Ray and I slept in a double bed but we made Shola sleep in the single because he wet himself a lot when he was a child. To be fair, he was two years younger and, after losing his mother, he must have been traumatised.

We were bundles of energy. Ray and I would imitate the wrestling stars of the day, like Mick McManus and Giant Haystacks, and have proper matches. Mum laughed because I took it all so seriously and hated getting beaten. She dressed the boys the same so people assumed Ray and I were twins. We resented it at first, but eventually got used to it. It was nice: we looked like a loving family. Family relationships are very important to me and especially so to Valerie. She's always played the big sister perfectly. When we were little she would bathe us, take us to the barbers, cook for us... everything.

As a toddler Val was my minder because I was always getting into scrapes. But one time I tripped and knocked my head on a wall, cutting my right eye badly. I've still got a scar there today. Val got smacked for not preventing my accident and, when no one was looking, she slapped me.

We loved it at John Burns Primary School in Battersea. When it was first built in the sixties it was considered state-of-the-art, being mostly glass, single-storey, completely open-plan and circular. There were no doors to separate the classrooms just insulated curtains. We thought we were in a spaceship. But the school was built to last just twenty years. It's pulled down now, and has moved to a more conventional brick building on two floors on Wyclisse Road.

The school was on the Dunston Estate so everyone knew each other and some of the mums, including ours, worked there as dinner ladies. There was a great sense of community. Even the teachers came round our houses socially once in a while. The sports master (Alistair Airey, a New Zealander) used to come for dinner and he loved mutton curry. Many of us from those days are still friends.

Mum always had at least two jobs. She cleaned, was a dinner lady at John Burns and juggled other jobs. I'm very close to Mum and don't mind admitting I was a clingy baby. So when, at two, she left Valerie and me with her cousin during the week to look after us whilst she went to work, we were very unhappy. We stayed in

Tooting Broadway and it must have been the most miserable five days of my short life because I threw her glasses down the stairs and smashed them in protest. She couldn't understand why I'd done that until Valerie explained. So she started taking me to a child-minder on her way to work before picking us up on the way home, around nine o'clock. But by then I was always asleep and waking us up to go home was not an ideal situation. Eventually, Mum made an arrangement with my godmother, who lived in the flat above us with her three daughters, to look after Val and me. It was great – no need to leave home and four playmates, albeit girls who had zero interest in football.

I was a happy kid at school. My best mates were Roger Parnell, Corrie Morris, Kevin Addison, Danny Rhodes, Paul 'Big Nose' Speller and Brendon Bartlett. Paul is still a close pal now and can remember stories about me better than I can! Mum says I was a good kid and even when I misbehaved I was always honest enough to own up. Like the time I ate all the ice cream. She lined the four of us up and asked who was responsible. When I admitted it so that the others wouldn't get punished as well she was impressed with my truthfulness. But I still got smacked.

Mum and Dad always believed I would get somewhere in sports. They took loads of my sports trophies to Jamaica when they moved back there, and Mum still has them displayed in her cabinet. For me, sport wasn't just an interest: it was an obsession. My metabolism was so fast that Mum took me to the doctor's twice because she was worried about my development. I didn't eat much, just milk and juice, and I was always thirsty. They did all kinds of tests on me and the doctors said I was fine – I just had a lot of energy to burn, which kept me small. Mum tried to build me up with solid Jamaican 'Yard' food and lots of eggs. Always the comedian, I used to make her laugh, especially by imitating the monkeys when the Typhoo Tea ads came on TV.

Watching and playing sport was my whole life then and the best way to annoy me was to stand in front of the TV when football was on. Dad used to encourage me to pick out the finer points in, say, a Viv Richards' swing or a Kenny Dalglish pass. Liverpool was the dominant team in the late seventies and I've supported them ever since. Playing for them was my boyhood dream. Snooker was a big passion, too. Mum bought us a little table and when it was too cold, wet or dark to play outside, we would amuse ourselves on it.

How Mum and Dad got through those times I don't know. Her first job was in a launderette in Angel, Islington. Then she worked for ten years as a supervisor at St Olive's Hospital in Bermondsey and later at the Victoria and Albert Museum as a cleaner. We used to enjoy going to see the exhibits and Mum sometimes took us to the Imperial War Memorial in Kennington. We were fascinated by those huge guns and tried to climb them, despite Mum's protests.

When he first came to England Dudley worked at the Birds Eye Food factory in the Old Kent Road before working in a carpet factory.

Cooking and domesticated stuff has never been my forté, partly because Mum spoilt me. When I learnt to fry eggs I was so frightened of getting burnt that I'd break them into the pan, then run and stand over on the other side of the kitchen until they were almost burnt. Mum thought it was hilarious. She didn't laugh, though, the day I forgot about my cooking. Aged ten, I was frying some eggs for a sandwich and heard the kids outside playing football. That was all the distraction I needed and I was out there in a flash. Mum had popped down the shops and luckily she came back just in time to ensure the fire brigade was not needed. Knowing my football obsession, she could see the funny side of it, despite me almost burning the house down.

People who know me now think I must have been a wild child but I was quite the opposite. Ray was the wild one. I took school very seriously, especially maths. That's because Dad used to drill it into me. He'd ask, 'How much thousand mek' a million?' If you couldn't answer him back straight away he'd say, 'You damn fool, you!' My siblings weren't so good at maths and Dad used to kill them with questions.

Even at seven my talent for football was already showing. I played with eleven-year-olds in central midfield in the school side. Scoring wasn't so important to me as being in the thick of it. I wanted to be more involved and create chances. But in those days cricket was really my favourite sport. I was an all-rounder and played for the A team. All the West Indies greats were my favourites – Viv Richards, Clive Lloyd, Michael Holding, Desmond Haynes, Gordon Greenidge and Malcolm Marshall – especially when Marshall smashed Mike Gatting on the nose!

Small for my age, I realised that if you paid attention to detail then you could improve more quickly, technique over power. Watching sportsmen on TV and practising for hours and hours, I would gradually improve. There was a very competitive streak in me that I still have to this day.

Most of us kids came from the Wickersley Estate. My teacher, Mr Airey, used to say to me, 'Jamie, you're not a great scholar, you can't sing, play guitar and will never stand out in the school play, but if you put your mind to it, you could make a career as a professional sportsman, probably football.' He believed in me so much that he sent me for football and cricket trials with Battersea schools. As things were tight at home he kindly bought me a pair of Mitre black boots with screw-in studs. I thought I was the bollocks! We all came from poor families who had to scrimp and save, and to have those boots really boosted my self-confidence. To this day I'm grateful to Mr Airey for that wonderful gesture. After away matches he even took us for treats in chip shops and Wimpeys.

Mr Airey was amazed at the length of my throw-ins, and he was furious at one confused teacher, who kept flagging me for foul throws because he couldn't believe a kid my size was doing it correctly. Parents and supporters at Battersea Park looked on in awe. Mr Airey reckons I still owe him 50p for the boots – hope he hasn't charged interest! He was surprised – and disappointed – when I ended up in jail but pleased to hear about me turning things round. He's 73 now and living back in New Zealand. 'Any time you're over here, there's always a bed here for you, James,' he said.

* * * * *

It was seeing what Mum and Dad had to go through to bring us up that made me look ahead to how hard it would be when I myself grew up. I used to think, 'I can't go through that.' That's partly why I went off the rails in my teens. We never went hungry, but there was that constant worry with money. At least we always had full-on West Indian cooking, which is not cheap. It was never burger and chips in our house. As a kid I never ate fish because West Indian dishes, like the vinegary fish dish escovitch, snapper and saltfish, seemed to have a million bones in them. Picking bones out of my mouth interfered with my sports time. I ate so fast, Mum used to say, 'Hey bwoy, you cut and swallow all the while. You never nyam your food properly!'

Like all West Indian households of that time, ours

was very disciplined. Everyone had to do chores. My parents would beat you for fun if the chores didn't get done. Ray used to enjoy it, but it never did anything for me. Punishment came in different ways, depending on how bad the offence. You could get the hand, slipper, curtain wire or belt. When you came to be punished, it was torture because they would send you off to get the instrument. If you couldn't find it, you'd get double! Curtain wire was the worst because you'd get welts. I used to put a book inside my trousers to protect myself and splashed water in my eyes to pretend I was crying.

But kids were tougher then than now and we were taught to always defend ourselves, no matter how big the other kid was, or how many of them there were. If we came home crying and admitted we hadn't hit the other kid back, we were sent out to defend ourselves. After a while, no one could take liberties with me. Paul Speller used to say, 'I wouldn't like to be on the end of your punch!'

I was eleven when I joined the Boy Scouts, and not long after we had a boxing competition. I'd never boxed before but, after watching Marvin Hagler on TV, I decided to go in for it. I had to fight Ray in the final. We agreed not to hurt each other but when he hit me with a sneaky 'haymaker', I gave him a left and right and he started bawling. I was getting aggressive then with strong, quick hands and very, very determined, maybe too headstrong...

Boxing has always been an interest and I can remember listening with Dad to the Alan Minter-Marvin Hagler fight on the radio. Minter was the British hero, the world middleweight champ. He'd won a bronze medal at the 1972 Olympics and the media tracked his career ever since he turned pro. But he had a big National Front following, which led to rumours that he was racist. When he announced at a press conference that he could never lose his title to a black man it caused a storm. We were furious and desperately wanted Hagler to win. The bald-headed American smashed Minter up in three rounds. It caused a riot at Wembley Arena with the racists claiming Hagler had butted the cut-up Minter, even though he won it fairly. Dudley was jumping around in his pyjamas. The cord on his pants came loose and fell down, but he was so happy, he just laughed.

Chapter 3

ROADRUNNER'S TOO FAST

In my childhood most of my mates were older than me, which probably led to me getting into trouble so early, wanting to impress them. At that time girls were not in my life. Sport was my only passion, especially the West Indies cricket team. I loved it when they did a blackwash on England, especially against Mike Gatting, who was horrible. We always had four quality pace bowlers in those days. It was relentless. At that time I loved football and cricket so much that I thought I could do both professionally, like Ian Botham – he's one of the few past sportsmen I respect.

It may surprise everyone to learn that I was a studious kid. I used to go home, do my homework and then go and play sport. But when it came to fights, I knew how to defend my corner. I only had six or seven fights throughout my school life, but I never lost. Two boys got bashed up on the same day in separate incidents. One of them, an Indian kid called Bollagee, was taking the piss out of me. The other was Keith O'Neill for something so trivial I can't even remember why. I gave them both black eyes and busted mouths. Both times it took just a couple of punches and then it was over. Maybe I should have been a boxer.

There was a horrible family on our estate called the Marnocks, who were always causing trouble. Aged nine, my most treasured possession was a cricket ball from a West Indies-England match at the Oval Dad had taken us to in 1979, a wicked experience. Having a signed ball was my happiest memory from that great day as the West Indies won the Test series 1-0 with four drawn, so it was another blackwash. We were playing with the ball, but Dean Marnock took it home, refusing to give it back. Ray and I went to his house and his father answered the door. He told us to go away, or he would set the dogs on us. He even threatened to call the police. Bastard!

Distraught and furious, I saw Dean out playing and decided to beat him up. He ran home, crying, and his mum came to our house and started giving Ray and me all this vicious racist abuse. Mum was coming back from the shops and heard her. She didn't ask any questions, just laid into her. Mum is petite, just a little piece, and the woman was much bigger, but Mum started beating her up. She only stopped when the woman started screaming. She ran home and got her husband to come to our house. He turned up with a screwdriver in his hand. Mum was scared but brave enough to call his bluff. She opened the door and told him to go away, or she would call the police. Mum reported them to Social Services and the local police station, and instructed a solicitor to write them a warning letter saying that she was prepared to take them to court. I got my ball back and they never troubled us again. The Marnocks tried to pre-empt the trouble they could have got into by telling Social Services that we were a nuisance family, but their reputation went before them. They were informed that if anybody was a nuisance family, they were. Years later I ended up beating Dean up again for taking a liberty: I had sold Dean something and he promised to pay me. Every time I bumped into him he had an excuse so after getting pissed off with his stalling, one day I gave him some lefts in his face. He must have thought, 'Boy, I don't want to get these like clockwork.' He paid up in full straight away.

Every week Mum used to take us to Sunday school at the Baptist Church on the Wandsworth Road. It was okay, but it cut into my sports time. As soon as I was big enough to make up my own mind, I stopped going. By now I was playing football on Sunday mornings for Larkhall Phoenix. Mum used to come to support us when she could, even on the coldest, wettest day. She is so loyal and I love her dearly.

Playing practical jokes is part of my character. Even

when I was a kid I was known for doing that. Val was always playing with my hair because it was naturally long and wavy. One day we played a great joke on Mum when she came home from work. She called Valerie down from upstairs and asked where I was. Val said she didn't know, but had a friend with her. I came down, wearing a wig, lipstick, handbag, earrings and stiletto heels. Mum asked, 'What mother allows her daughter to dress up like that? Who is your mother, girl?' Val and I couldn't help but laugh, and that's when she realised who it was.

Mum is a very astute woman. She has two houses in Mandeville, in Jamaica's parish of Manchester. She bought one and built the other. The one she doesn't live in is reserved for when her extensive family visits, that's how thoughtful and caring she is. In Jamaica she is treated as a celebrity's mum and gets a lot of requests for money. Often she gives, but not too often, otherwise people take advantage. Mum is very independent and when I offer to help financially she always refuses. 'No, son, you've got your own children and responsibilities,' she says. But when I do give her money, she is always thankful.

I was very respectful to the police in those days. Scared of them, in fact. To this day Valerie still laughs about the time when I was twelve and a police car stopped beside us. I started running for no reason. That made everyone else start to run. They searched me. It was in the days after the Brixton riots and dubious suss laws – the hated suspicion laws when the police could stop and search you if they suspected you of anything illegal, though consensus had it that we black youths were routinely harrassed for being black. Healthy black people used to get arrested, end up dead in custody and after months of investigations no one was to blame. No wonder I ran! That uniform used to get me paranoid. But I had good reason because the police round our way used to be bad. Post-Brixton riots they beat a man up for fun. The worst thing we used to do was to throw things at people or cars. Eggs, stones, fruit... Great fun.

From eleven to fourteen I had a paper round and did a 'Pardner' (savings plan amongst West Indians) of £5 a week. Once a year I got £260 – a fortune. It would go on a big shopping spree.

I didn't get involved in gangs until my mid-teens. Partly because of boredom we started thieving mopeds and, for a laugh, we also used to pick fights with drunken men coming out of pubs. Mum was still strict even though I thought I was a bad boy. She really kept me on my toes. There was the time when she embarrassed me by coming out with a cricket bat. 'James,' she shouted. 'Get your backside inna' de yard! What you doing out on de road at dis' time of night?' The shame of it...

By now we weren't scared of the police anymore and started taunting them, again partly out of boredom. They'd come round looking for trouble and we'd give them a hard time, especially the black ones, who we called 'Judas'. At that time the police had all sorts of street names: 'Cockroach', 'Bull', 'Raddicks'. Now we call them 'the Feds'. Some of them were okay, but a few were vicious bastards. There was a particularly ruthless one who I remember to this day. You could tell he was going places in the force because he was so mean. He's gone up the ranks since then and is in plain clothes now. I've seen him on TV – he's in the murder squad. I remember how, at seventeen, I bumped into him in Clapham Junction and he said, 'I know what you're up to and I'm gonna come and kick off your front door.' But he had no evidence: he was out of order.

There was another one that we called 'Road-runner' because we could never out-run him. He was fast as lightning, like the cartoon character. When he came on the scene you knew you were in trouble. I stayed out of Roadrunner's way. No one used to give it to him.

We then started breaking into cars and nicking stereos. To pull the stereos out, we had special keys, and you could get £40 for cheap ones and up to £80 for the better makes like Blaupunkt, Pioneer and Sony. With the money we bought clothes. Very stylish I was – Biscote jeans, C17 jeans, Diamond trousers, Pringle, Lyle & Scott, Farrah, and the trainers had to be ZX, Torsion. If you've got them, you're the man.

I wasn't the most stylish 'cos there were boys doing

more cars and more clothes. Sport was still an obsession, too. I never smoked, drank or did drugs. To this day I've never smoked a cigarette nor tried weed – it has just never appealed. But I do love my Guinness.

* * * * *

At eleven, I went to the Sir Walter St John's Secondary School in Battersea High Street. It was just another inner-city school with the usual mix of kids from diverse backgrounds. At fourteen I had my first romantic encounter: Samantha Whitby. She dumped me after two weeks with no explanation. I was gutted, really distraught. I was feeling her man! We even bought each other a ring. I remember she wouldn't go past first base, just kissing. We were very naïve. At that time I actually wasn't much into girls – they didn't even come a close second to sport!

In many cases, I believe getting into trouble has nothing to do with your environment. For some, they choose ghetto life. None of my siblings got into trouble – I was the only one. Youths around Battersea now, I see them going that way. They're not just picking up knives, but guns. It's a lack of dedication, or things have conspired against them. But I've learnt that you get nothing in life without hard work.

Larkhall Phoenix was managed by Pete Rhodes, whose son Danny was a star player. I also played for Heathbrook after school. Professional teams watched me, but no one made a move: they all said the same thing – I was too small. I had two trials at Crystal Palace at fifteen and later Fulham and Millwall, but it never worked out. At Palace I thought I had done well in centre-midfield, but the size issue came up again. I was advised to drink Guinness to put weight on. At first I hated it – too bitter – but I suffered in silence and now I love it. The only other kid who made it from my year was Kevin Campbell, who signed for Arsenal. He played for Arnside from Brixton and scored all their goals. They won the league and beat us 1-0 in the Cup Final. Frank Sinclair is two years younger than me. He's also from our way and made it too, at Chelsea.

Danny Rhodes was a year younger than me and because we got on so well, Pete treated me like his own son. He liked the fact that I looked out for Danny when he started at the same secondary school. Pete really knew the game well. He encouraged good football and had a very professional attitude, even for us kids. We were the only team I knew of who did proper drills. He used to run us into the ground but I prided myself on always being the fastest.

Ray used to impress Pete, too, because he would finish just behind me, still looking fresh. But Pete got suspicious and sussed out what he was doing. Ray would start off running with us, then duck into a shop doorway to have a smoke. He would only join in when I had almost finished.

Pete is a taxi driver and Danny, too. Pete would pick us up after school with Danny and drop us home in his black cab. He called us his two black sons. We were so close that, when Mum and Dad went back to Jamaica, Pete invited me to go and live with him. There was a time when the school caretaker was abusing Ray. Pete told him off. 'Who are you?' asked the caretaker. 'I'm his dad!' shouted Pete. The caretaker got killed by a juggernaut soon after and all the kids said, 'See what happens when you mess with Pete.' After that, he was treated with even more respect.

Pete liked me because despite being the best player, I was always willing to listen and practise anything he suggested. For example, he told me to improve my left foot 'cos it was a little weak, so I worked on that. When Pete gave me advice in front of the team, instead of throwing a tantrum I would nod and try to correct it the next time. He believed in me so much that he once wrote to Chelsea asking for a trial. They agreed to play us in Battersea and although I played well, they picked a kid who had barely got into our team. Gutted again.

After school we used to have really competitive games in the playground and one of the teachers, Eduardo D'Orey, used to join in. In his twenties, he was Spanish, and he took his football really, really seriously. He would steam into tackles like Vinnie Jones. Pete Rhodes used to join in and when Mr

D'Orey made a crunching tackle, sending a kid sprawling, he would smile and ask, 'What about that then, Pete?' I always had to be the best and Pete was amazed that even in 'kick and run' games I could ghost past kids. Pete was very special to me, used to buy boots or give me money if I didn't have enough. That's why I always made an effort to scrape together enough at Christmas to buy him a present.

At fourteen I was so obsessed with football that I'd play four or five times over the weekend. Pete could see that I was suffering, looking tired and jaded, and advised me to play just once. I took his advice and shone after that: I was player of the year for Larkhall Phoenix twice running. Pete put us in a league in Battersea in 1980. There were three divisions and he wanted us to play in the top one, but those wise officials at the Battersea Association League said we had to go in the bottom one. We won every game by ridiculous scores like 25-0. I was sometimes scoring eight or nine goals. That first season we only lost once, to Arnside.

Then, for the next two years, we went in the Shirley and District League. We won all our games easily, but we were also proud of the fact that we got the Most Sporting Team of the Year award because we always treated our opponents with respect whilst thrashing them. We were known for fair play and the only time one of our boys did a rough tackle on someone, almost breaking his leg, Pete made sure he apologised afterwards, not only to the boy, but also his dad and all the officials. Pete instilled a discipline in me, which I still retain today.

He never showed any bias. Once, he dropped Ray and me for five games because we looked tired. Disappointed, I never complained, and even turned up for matches to watch. There was a real bond between us and although Pete had heard that I was going off the rails, he always treated me well. He liked the fact that when a new kid joined the team, I always made him feel welcome; he also liked my temperament on the field. If I was fouled, I would never retaliate but would make sure I made a dummy of the guy for the rest of the match.

Those were great days. One time we lost to a team, mainly because our big, black centre-forward was useless – he missed seven or eight easy chances. We played them again the next week, but this time our striker was Kevin Campbell, who was already at Arsenal and shouldn't really have been playing for us. Pete heard their manager in the dressing room saying, 'They've got a big centre-forward, but don't worry, he's crap!' From thirty yards out with the minimum of backlift Campbell scored our first goal and we won 7-0. Yours truly got two and Campbell hit a hat trick. Near the end, their manager asked Pete, 'Couldn't you have played your reserves?' Pete laughed and said, 'These *are* my reserves!'

My fitness and running ability was a personal pride

so when one day Pete challenged me to a 400-metres race round a track, I thought there could only be one winner – but he won. I wanted a rematch, but he didn't fancy it and said he wanted to rest on his laurels. He still owes me that rematch. I think Pete Rhodes could have made it as a proper manager. He really believed in me and always said, 'You can make it.' When he took me to the Palace trials I was very nervous, but as soon as I started I was okay. By the end of the second trial, when they rejected me again, I doubted myself, but I never gave up hope.

Because of the politics Pete disbanded Larkhall Phoenix in 1985 when I was fifteen. As puberty kicked in, fights on the pitch reduced the fun element, so I joined another team, Palace Guard. Pete was part of the management team. He played me as a sweeper, which was a masterstroke because I was more comfortable there, but I liked to get involved in centre-midfield so went back to that position.

* * * * *

At fifteen I went for trials with Surrey Cricket Club. Some trial! It was only in the nets. I knew I had little chance because most of the players came from private teams and enjoyed playing on the best pitches in the best kit. Even though the club is based at The Oval, in the heart of a working-class area, in those days kids like me from that kind of background had a slim chance of making it. Despite being better at cricket than football, because I didn't have the support system, my chances were virtually nil.

Not knowing what I was going to do after school, it was nice to get some work experience in the Barclays Bank in Lavender Hill for a couple of months. I was only paid £20 a week and always gave it all to Mum. She didn't want to take it, but I insisted. Mum would put some in a savings account that she started for me. Money was tight in the house, but Mum and Dad made it a point of duty to always give us pocket money. I used to get a fiver for the weekend. We never went without and were always well fed.

After leaving school I joined Old Sinjuns, a team formed from my old school mates. John Sackett was manager of the fourth XI. The first time he saw me play he thought I was special so when he took over the first XI he immediately put me in with grown men. When I got arrested for my first offence at seventeen John wrote a letter to the court as a character reference. He got me trials at Fulham and Millwall and even gave me an apprentice mechanic's job at his garage. He believed in me proper. I also played for his Wednesday side. Nothing happened at the trials but it wasn't for lack of trying on John's part. When I got arrested at nineteen there was no way could he help me out. I owe a lot to John Sackett.

In the summer of 1987 I left school to attend Westminster College and do a physical Education

Theory course, and that's when I really found out about women. I started meeting older people at college, but was socialising more than attending classes. After eight months, I got thrown out 'cos I was bunking off to see a girl called Anna. But she gave me the runaround. Anna was the hottest chick around. Part-Spanish and beautiful, she left men hanging. I remember I had one slow dance with her and thought, 'She likes me!' I felt teased – I didn't even get a kiss.

In my short time at college my best friends were Michael Allman, Chris Lamby, Michael, Susan and someone who fancied me called Elizabeth. She frightened me – she was so hungry. She weren't the best looker – I was not brave enough to risk my street cred. Mum didn't find out I'd been thrown off the course until she got a letter saying that because of my continued absence I was no longer registered. She tried to persuade me to attend, but the college refused to take me back. What I hadn't told her was that they tried to get me to clean toilets at one point as punishment for my absence. She was furious when she found out.

Maria took my virginity. It wasn't in the most romantic of places, on the floor in an alleyway, actually. So in a way she could say that the earth moved for her. Then we went to a party after. I couldn't get enough of her and I must have done something right 'cos she was on my case for more. Maria was pretty, blonde with a nice figure. I can't remember if her eyes were blue; wasn't looking there. We saw each other a few more times but then it was my turn to do the dumping – I wanted a taste of someone else. I thought, 'Look what I've been missing!' Maria wanted us to carry on but let's just say it ended anyway. By this time, Natasha Tilbury, who would become my little boy Nathan's mum, was on the scene, too. She played games as well. They were coming in thick and fast, and I was only eighteen! Tasha was only fifteen and her parents didn't approve of me being a bit older and having a rep'. I couldn't go round there and knock on her door so I used to throw pebbles up to her bedroom window. But one day I threw a stone too hard and broke the window. Her old man was furious.

Lisa Nicholls was my next girlfriend, but that only lasted three weeks 'cos I was on the rebound. She's still with her next man to this day and they have two kids. I'd been chasing Natasha. She, too, was playing games – gave me lips and nothing else. Natasha saw me with Lisa, got jealous and started crying on me. 'You know I like you,' she said.

Natasha was a virgin and I broke her virginity at the top of a block of flats. Natasha's brother used to hang around with me, but once I started seeing her, he switched. One day we were having an argument over her standing me up. Her friend ran to her house and her brother came running out. Without finding out what was going on, he punched me in the face. I butted him and broke his nose. He was the London 100 metres champion and you should have seen him run back to his house. His old man came out with his wife and she called me a black bastard. 'Yeah, I might be a black bastard, but your daughter loves me,' I replied. Then she tried to hit me with a stiletto. Friends pulled me away from fighting the dad. That was the start of me getting really bad...

* * * * *

I was seventeen and moving with a few older boys from the Dunston Wall, the boundary of our estate. One boy, Paul Legitt, had a car and he was always mugging me off by leaving me behind. There was a time at my friend Ann Warren's house when he said something to me that was out of order. I responded, 'Mind I come over and rob you.' I flicked out my knife, held it to his throat and took all his money and a big bag of puff. I thought he was a pussy-hole: he wasn't a proper bad boy, he was working and just buying friends.

It was a slippery slope for me from there. All the bad boys used to report back to me when they nicked stuff and paid into my one-man protection racket. I even made them thieve for me and took all their cash, it was like a 'tax' on the bad boys. So, what did they get for their weekly retainer? I saved them from a beating...

Someone tried to set me up at the snooker hall in Wandsworth Road. A pussy called Frank was running up his mouth so I nicked his cue. His old man was a gangsta. He phoned and said, 'I hear you think you're a bad man – give my son the cue back.' But I didn't. Me, Paul Speller and one of my other mates had letters sent to our houses. Mine simply said, 'The people you hang around with can't help you'. Soon after, two men were coming towards me and one asked for the time. The other pulled out a baseball bat. He hit me in the eye as I grabbed the other one and used him as a shield. I ran to get one of my mates, but by the time I got back they had gone. We never saw Frank in the snooker hall again.

In my teens Dean Johns was one of my best mates. He was two years younger, but a big kid with plenty of bottle. The incident that really bonded us was the time when one of our Dunston Road crew started a row with someone from another gang and things got out of hand. About twelve of us were waiting for them with baseball bats when two carloads turned up. But they were grown men in their twenties with machetes. The kid they came for ran off; our mob ran, too. But Dean and I stood firm. We didn't stand a chance, but a lot of pride was at stake here. We were shitting ourselves. Their leader said, 'You two are a bit brave, aren't you?' Then they drove off.

Dean and I had lots of punch-ups and never lost once. Mostly, it started with people being pricks and looking for trouble, but looking back we were usually half to blame because of the flash way we were dressed and having a proper laugh. It wound some people up. (Dean turned out all right. He lives in a leafy part of Surrey now and has his own company.)

One night Dean and me were in the Theatre Nightclub in Wandsworth when two chaps started trouble. They were just two little pricks, but one of them got his mate, who turned out to be this gigantic black guy – enormous! When there's trouble I'm not the type to start shouting and swearing, I start talking softly. I invited the big guy to come and sort it outside, but he lost his nerve and refused.

Another time in the theatre there was this arguing going on. I went to the toilet... and there was the guy who started the trouble in the first place. I banged him out. They had to call an ambulance. There were all these Feds looking for me and, driving home, I knew they would stop me. So I parked up and went to a warehouse in Kember Road, Wandsworth. The owners could tell I was a rogue, but they let me stay for a couple of hours until it all died down. My career as a hoodlum had truly started.

Chapter 4

HELD FOR MURDER

Being arrested on suspicion of murder is no fun. The police said someone had been thrown off a balcony on the Patmore Estate in Battersea and, unluckily for me, I was walking through the estate about the time it happened. The victim was a friend and I'd been hanging around with him until the day he died. Even though I could tell they realised I had nothing to do with it, they still questioned me for hours.

It was a horrible experience, particularly for an seventeen-year-old kid, because three Feds turned up at my house when I was out. When I got home Mum and Dad said they were looking for me, so when they came back, it was no great surprise. I found out what it was for, though, and I got scared. They took me into Battersea Police Station for questioning and left me to stew in a cell for an hour or two. It was frightening.

Race relations were still appalling then. Even though it was six years after the Brixton riots, it was only two years after the Broadwater Farm riot in Tottenham when PC Keith Blakelock was attacked by a mob, allegedly of black youths. Up to now the case has never been solved so all the Feds at that time had bare hatred for the man on the street. That's why they wanted to nab me I reckon.

I was there for about five or six hours, but it seemed like a lifetime. In the end they let me go. Of all the trouble I've ever been in, the worst part is being in a police cell. They are cold and boring, and your mind is working overtime thinking about what they're going to do to you. In those days black people got killed in cells and the perpetrators were never held accountable. At that time I was wild and enjoyed a tear-up, but fighting and nicking car stereos was my limit, not badness like that.

When they tried to arrest me once for something I can't remember, Paul Speller advised me to go quietly and coaxed me into the police car. They were so sure I was going quietly, that they'd got me, that they weren't prepared for me to jump out of the other side and run off. One copper caught hold of my top, but I just wriggled out of his grasp and sprinted off to shouts of, 'You black bastard!' Speller would always back me up in a tight situation, even though he was not naturally aggressive. Once I got in an argument at the Queen's pub in Battersea with a known troublemaker while playing snooker. His mates jumped me and draipsed me up against a wall. One pulled out a machete as four tried to hold me still. Machete Man was about to do me when Speller arrived like the cavalry. He shouted, 'Shut your eyes, Jamie!' then sprayed them all in the eyes with CS gas. Through half-open eyes, coughing my guts out, I started knocking them about for fun.

Trouble seemed to follow me everywhere, even when I hadn't done a single thing. One time when I was living with a girl in her flat in Latchmere Road, Battersea, I was suspected of an attempted murder just because witnesses said the bloke who done it had funky dreads like me. It was even in the local papers. I didn't want to do bird for something that I hadn't done so every morning I would leave at six to stay with a bredren in north London. One night we had a little drink-up in my girl's flat and they were all puffing strong, Ganja everywhere. When everyone had left, I was in bed, naked with my girl, when we heard a knock on the door. I peeped through the curtains and saw Paul Speller in handcuffs with two Feds beside him. I was so scared that, without thinking, I jumped out of the back window and climbed onto the roof butt naked. If anyone had seen me they would have been shocked initially, then probably dialled 999. It was a freezing cold night and the police were questioning my girl for ages on whether or not Speller had been at the party. They had found an empty bag of weed on him and wanted to check that he wasn't a dealer. Speller got off with a caution but my frozen t'ings took a week to thaw out!

It was around that time that things became as bad as they possibly could. I was staying at Valerie's in Battersea and neither of us ever had any money. Once I'd been out all night drinking and had only one hour's sleep. The next day I want to the local snooker hall. It was a Saturday and my money was running out. Dean Johns was with me and as we were leaving, I told him to go outside and I'd see him in a minute. He went outside. I busted the till and took the cash (about £70 or £80) out of it and picked up a video recorder that was being used in the snooker hall, really cool and casual. Out the back, the staff was making sandwiches. As I was walking out, the manager came out and, because he knew me, he said to just put it all back and it would go no further. I thought about it, but beat him up instead, partly because I was embarrassed and also because I needed the dough. I got away with the stuff but knew it was only a matter of time because they all knew me. I sold the recorder straight away for £60.

About ten days later I got arrested at Val's. I was a human crime wave in those days and got done for three other robberies and one assault. At that time in my bad boy days things were so bad that, after missing the last train home from Clapham Junction to Val's in Croydon, I was desperate. It was the 11.10pm train and as I ran up to the platform, it pulled away. It was a horrible feeling, it seemed to sum up everything that was going wrong for me. That night I'd been with Tasha and when you're enjoying yourself, you lose track of time. I had nowhere to stay and was forced to sleep overnight in a broom cupboard in Battersea. The youths in the area had their own little place to hang out and smoke ganja out of sight of the police and neighbours who might report them. As all of them still lived at home they couldn't smoke it there so they needed some space for themselves – the broom cupboard. I slept on a chair in the broom cupboard. But I checked myself. 'You know what, this ain't the one,' I thought. 'I've got more integrity than this.'

At 6.30am the police came, banging on the door like they were really important. I knew what was coming and I'm a great believer in thinking that you should always mentally prepare yourself for anything. The three plain-clothed cops cuffed me. One of them was the officer who later joined the murder squad, who I said earlier I'd never forget, who had warned me that time in Clapham Junction, and his sergeant. They charged me and I was in court the next morning. I managed to get £1,000 bail, which Valerie kindly put up. They told me to come back the next day at 2pm. That's when I knew I'd be held on remand because they thought I'd interfere with witnesses.

They sent me to Feltham and I had untold emotions

on the way: 'Boy, you've really gone and done it now.'
But I already knew I had friends there. I know it was
silly but I hoped Mum and Dad wouldn't find out. No
matter how much you think you're bad, your mum's
the one who brought you up, wiped your dirty bottom
and all that, and you don't want her to know. I was
three months on remand. One of my co-defendants,
Rats, was in there, too. I was given three years at
Kingston Crown Court. It must be the worst court in
the land – every man gets bird there. I didn't think I
deserved it.

It was my first offence and all the circumstances
revealed that Mum and Dad left me, I had no money
and was a talented footballer. I'd tried to work as a
mechanic, but the pay was a joke. The £50 wages was
done too quickly. Feltham is the worst place for
rehabilitating a youth. Everyone tries to prove himself
in there. In a way it's like the film *Scum*. You're bound
to get into an argument in there, it's a gladiator
mentality. I didn't because I had at least one of my
people on every wing so no one troubled me.

Feltham was all regimented, like being in the army.
We'd get up at eight and have to arrange our beds,
then wash in a sink before breakfast. The toughest
warden was Mr Towers, aka 'Mr T'. He was the
physical education instructor, big and strong, and
whenever there was serious trouble they would send
him in there first. Football was a welcome relief – they
would send in teams to play us.

We were well catered for, but the canteen was a joke – it was more like a servery in a Victorian factory. You'd get porridge, of course, and a little egg or a sausage. One or the other, never both. We were growing youths so that type of food was totally inadequate. After breakfast we were banged up again. At weekends we'd get 'association' in the afternoon and evening sometimes, a chance to relax and socialise with the other inmates. Occasionally we'd get a morning association. I used to try to tire myself out. Morning break from our cells was at 10.30 when, if we were lucky, we would play pool for an hour. It all depended on how much staff they had.

Lunch was always meat with potatoes, usually roasted or mashed. You only got chips on a Friday with fish. At least when I was in a regular prison, the food was okay – it had to be half-decent otherwise there would have been a riot. But you could tell there was no love put into it, unlike Mum's. Seasoning? Forget it!

I met Junior 'Luton' Atkinson when I first went to Feltham in 1990. It was a very historic time because that weekend Nelson Mandela was released from jail after 27 years and Mike Tyson was sensationally knocked out by Buster Douglas in the biggest upset in boxing history. I was barely able to take in these events as my head was spinning from being incarcerated. Short and stocky, Luton was in for Aggravated Bodily Harm, stealing, receiving stolen goods and other things. I didn't speak to him much. Being from Luton, I kept with my bredrens from London, especially Rats. If you didn't come from London you were known as a country bumpkin. Luton knew that and he kept his head down. He noticed that most of the trouble usually started in arguments about whose turn it was next at the pool table. After a while Luton got comfortable enough to start playing. But because he came from the country, the other men started taking liberties. Luton took it for a while, but one day he erupted. He hit one guy and bit another on the ear. From that day everyone said, 'Don't fuck with Luton.'

Like many other inmates, for me the gym was a welcome release from boredom and stress. When I first went in, I could only bench press 35 kilos, which is about 80 lb. But I found it hard. From that day I started doing press-ups in my cell because the others were pressing enormous weights. After three months I was pressing the same as them. We'd be in our cells between four and six, and then watch a little TV in the evenings – *EastEnders* and films. Dinner was at five – white man's time – and you didn't get anything till the next morning. Having dinner so early was hard for the black guys because we're used to eating much later. My favourite was stew, but the cooks obviously just flung anything into it.

I was transferred to Brixton as soon as I was convicted three months later, then transferred to

Dover, a prison for young offenders. For me, one of the biggest differences between Feltham and Dover was that at Feltham we could have our cell lights on for as long as we liked, but in Dover lights off was ten o'clock sharp. Dover was an under-21 prison. At least it was better than Brixton where you had to go to the toilet in front of your cellmate. That was rough.

Paul Speller came to Dover with Tasha to see me. Luton's girl was Tracy. They're still together now and have two lovely kids. Tracy treated me like a brother and I'll always be grateful. Val used to send what they could afford, but if Tracy sent £10 to Luton, she would say that £5 was mine. We could only receive a maximum of £20 a week each which was mainly for phone cards. We had a system where we would live on the little money I got, and put Luton's away and build it up. He was working in the garden and earning better than me. Then after a few weeks when my money had run out we would survive on Luton's money and maybe have a little party. It worked well and helped us get through our sentences more easily.

There was a drama there when a mate called Danny was banged up for allegedly raping a girl. Some inmates wanted to beat him up, but I stopped it because I knew Danny was innocent.

* * * * *

Going to prison doesn't deter you from re-offending. When your belly's hungry, what you gonna do? I'm not illiterate, like many inmates. I had intelligence and could have been punished in a better way. Prison is supposed to rehabilitate you, but that's bullshit. The stigma of being banged up worsens your chances of getting on in life. That's why I feel the way I do about getting bird. If my parents had been there, things might have been different. I saw how they suffered financially too much and didn't want that for my own family.

I didn't really get to know Luton until we were both sentenced and sent to Dover. We sat together in the coach. It was a hot, sunny day and we ended up doing everything together. I was on Sandwich wing and he was on Deal wing. Mine was a tough wing, but Luton had all the quiet, sweet boys and soon decided to become the 'daddy'. Soon his cell was so full with crisps, phone cards and biscuits the inmates had to buy them back off him on 'double bubble' – twice as much as they had paid or exchanged them for. That's when he got transferred to my wing and we ended up sharing a cell. We bonded straight away, played lots of pool and snooker, but I always won. Luton thought I was good enough to be a snooker pro.

There was a tall, black kid there called Ebanks, who was like the screws' pet. He used to make them cups of tea and run errands for them. We hated him. I wasn't a troublemaker, but not an arse-licker either.

Ebanks didn't like me because when I beat him in sport, I'd try to humiliate him, like seven-ball him in pool [potting all my balls first] or nutmeg him in football. I liked to embarrass people with my skill, to make them a laughing stock. Luton said, 'James, when God was giving out talent he must have singled you out for extras.'

Luton was already in a bad mood the day he got knocked back at a parole hearing near the end of 1990. Then Ebanks upset him. Luton wanted to smash him up and I was ready to back him up even though it would have jeopardised my parole. But Luton told me to go before I got into trouble, too. The screws broke it up before it got out of hand.

We had some mad times, but the boredom and frustration at being banged up for twelve hours a day was hell. I used to escape by imagining I was doing the normal routine people outside take for granted when they've got their freedom. Luton woke up one Friday night thinking I had really lost it. I was pouring with sweat, dancing to jungle and house music playing on Radio Invicta. My reasoning was that if I couldn't get out to party, I might as well bring the party in. At that precise moment, it was the best rave anywhere in the world. There was a puddle of sweat around the spot where I was dancing to what Luton called my 'mad music'.

For a laugh, and to ease the boredom, we wrote to *The Voice* newspaper's sweethearts column, hoping at least to have pen pals and maybe have our egos boosted. I'm sure the girls who replied were lovely people, but all of them were so huge that we never answered any of them.

Luton became fed up of being second best to me at football and snooker. His only satisfaction was when we played cards. He usually won. One night he was beating me at Blackjack. Being so competitive, I just refused to give up, even though I must have owed him about a zillion packets of biscuits. Hours after, when he wanted to turn in for the night, I refused to let him sleep, determined to turn my luck around. By 4am we decided to call it quits and Luton decided to settle for just three packets of biscuits. He claims I still owe him a factory-size quantity of McVitie's!

Luton once got £20 unexpectedly and managed to sneak in a bottle of Captain Morgan's. We got really drunk that night and ended up almost fighting. I can't remember why.

Luton's volatile temperament could flare at any time. We loved playing football for Dover's prison side. After one match I went to get my lunch and heard a commotion at the servery. Luton was starving and they tried to give him a tiny piece of chicken that was no bigger than a mouse – it could well have been a mouse. When they refused to serve him a bigger piece, Luton started chucking pool balls at them. He went to the block [solitary confinement] for seven days.

It was no shock when I got my parole first time in

February 1991 – I had been a shining example of rehabilitation and rules were relaxed about football, where I was able to further demonstrate my good behaviour. That's despite all the little runnings me and Luton were getting up to. A guy called Donny was in Dover with us, doing a longer sentence: five years. Luton got out at around the same time as me, but being young and foolish, we didn't learn...

A year later Luton was listening to his radio in prison and heard about a prisoner at Camp Hill, who was attracting a lot of attention for his football ability. He guessed straight away who it was. When the name was confirmed on the radio his heart sank. Leaving Dover I was full of regret and good intentions, but my life was heading down a very slippery slope.

Chapter 5

GET ME OUT OF HERE!

I came out of Dover in February 1991 and had three months before trouble hit me again. By the end of May I was on remand at Wormword Scrubs. My mate Freddie had a fight with Yankee. I had an on-going beef with Yankee from two years earlier. He was five years older, a big man. Freddie said he'd been having arguments with Yankee.

It was on the Gideon Estate in Battersea. Yankee was walking past when Freddie started on him, knowing I would back him up. There were a lot of people around watching. Freddie was battling this guy, but not doing well. He was struggling. So when I stepped in to sort Yankee out, he tried to drop foot and run. But not many get away from me. We ended up outside a pub called The Crown and Yankee tried to run upstairs. The fool got himself caught really because there are steps leading up to The Crown but he chose to follow the zigzagging disabled ramp. How he thought that was the quickest route I don't know. Yankee got proper licks. Whilst I was licking him in the ribs, I tried to pull his bracelet off. I managed this, and the jacket came off, too. There was some money in there. Not much, but enough to buy drinks for the night.

I thought that was the end of the matter. But Yankee and his people put the word out that they were going to kill me. I thought, 'I'll have to deal with it because the problem won't just go away.' I was still skinny them times and it must have hurt Yankee's pride that a younger, smaller man had dealt with him. Yankee got brave and started saying he was looking for me. I knew where he lived on the Dunston Estate, so I waited one morning for him to go to work. I jumped out on him, saying, 'I heard say you were looking for me.' He ran off, then called the police. And that's after running up his big, brave mouth. Nothing to worry about, I thought, I've got Freddie on my side. Fearing arrest, I went on the run.

I'd tried to sign on and do the right thing after coming out of Dover but after five weeks it was impossible. You only got a giro for £60 every two weeks. Val tried to look after me, but it was tough. She had the baby, Aiysha, and money was tight. Times were so hard that I felt compelled to resort to my old ways. There was a new craze: bust the till in a shop, grab the money and run. Those times you only had to press a button on the till and it would open with all the 'paper' laid out like a buffet just waiting you to scoop it up. I went in the shop with a bredren and between us we grabbed £500. I had it on my toes straight away. No one was going to catch me. Nice little touch. Something told me to tuck the £250 under the sole of my trainers. The Feds were on it immediately, cars screeching around Battersea. As a helicopter circled, a black woman saw me hiding in her garden and called me into the house. Police knocked on her door. She denied I was in there but they knew 'cos the chopper had told them.

They arrested the woman, which I felt really bad about, and took us to Union Grove station nearby. She got cautioned and released. Them times police stations didn't really communicate with each other, which was great for me because Battersea wanted me for the Yankee case. Union Grove should have checked and never let me out. And to show you how stupid they were, my £250 remained safely in my trainers. They searched, but not well enough. No wonder they can't catch anyone. Had they arrested me, it would actually have been a relief. At that point I'd decided to turn myself in. I couldn't sign on, couldn't work. All that juggling was getting a bit too much.

To my surprise, Freddie grassed me up on the Yankee fight. If he hadn't, I would probably have got off as Yankee was seen as an unreliable witness. He was so volatile that he walked out of the dock three times. If not for Freddie, the case would have been thrown out of court. The jury would never have believed Yankee. My solicitor, Jill Buxton from Matillers, was brilliant and she tore into him. Jill was a white lady, based in Electric Avenue, Brixton, aged around forty, but she knew the coup. She was very understanding, but advised me to stay out of trouble. Val got Jill for me.

Jill was not judgmental. 'Can't you get into something else like sex?' she once asked. I was surprised and felt a bit embarrassed 'cos she was an older woman. But she had a point. I was just finding out about it, and what I had. I already knew it wasn't a normal package. I used to whip it out and the girls would say, 'Fucking hell! That ain't going nowhere near me!'

*****

The first time I went to jail I pleaded guilty because I had too much on me. Both trials were at Kingston Crown Court and it was the same Judge McCrae. He had a terrible reputation. Every man who came from Clapham Junction got bird.

The second time I pleaded not guilty because I wanted to see Freddie in the dock. I was sure he would back me and the case would be dismissed. He was in the dock for one and a half days and told them everything as if I started it. I was devastated – I thought he was kosher because we'd grown up together, but leading up to the trial I thought Freddie would switch. I knew the Feds were looking for me, so I didn't stay with Val. One time I saw them waiting for me outside her place. Plain clothes, but I recognised licence plates ending in LHX, so I ducked them. Some detectives! Everyone knew they were Feds, even in plain clothes – must have trained at the Inspector Clouseau School of Law Enforcement.

I was hiding out at my mate Danny Price's in nearby Battersea. Freddie came round and said he'd been arrested for the Yankee incident but assured me he would not grass. The next day they knocked on Danny's door. I had seen them approaching the house and hid in the bedroom. The cops were so useless they only searched the bedroom I had been sleeping in, the same room I had spoken to Freddie in. That's when I knew Freddie must have tipped them off. He got charged, but got off after pleading not guilty. I didn't go in the dock, never do – these lawyers know how to trip you up, no matter how innocent you are. Being driven to court, I was in a sweat box. It was a hot summer's day and after months on remand I was on my way to Lavender Hill Magistrates' Court before it went to trial at Kingston. We passed Freddie, walking there with a can of Tennant's in his hand. He looked like he didn't have a care in the world. I'd been on remand for three months in Wormwood Scrubs, then Brixton for four months.

It was a pretty uneventful time in Scrubs apart from the five-a-side game the screws (who were a nasty lot) arranged. They were coming like the Mean Machine and they tried to kick the fuck out of me. Bare hatred. Some of my team wanted to kick them back. Not me. I didn't retaliate, just used my skills to embarrass them with nutmegs (through their legs) and sending them for pies (making them go the wrong way). When you're playing against people who are locking you up every night, it's not hard to get motivated. We won 11-4 and I scored five. Everyone went mental. I got big props. In a funny way, that match gave me as much satisfaction as any professional triumph. To put it into context, some screws were evil. You just wanted to have it with them but knew it wasn't worth it. The young, black screws were the worst. One told me that I was heading for the lifers' wing. The little wanker said, 'I read your records and you're going over there soon.' I wanted to chin him and make them gwan. I was past caring anyway, my crew were gaining a reputation for being a formidable force not be messed with. The screws are the ones doing life. What a limited career, just locking people up every day. Most of them are Uncle Toms anyway. Their kind of attitude made things worse for people who genuinely wanted to turn their life round.

Certain folks look at people from the ghetto and assume the worse. I had a stable family and a decent education, but after Mum and Dad went to Jamaica I went off the rails. Some men from the ghetto don't have stable families and education, and for them doing crime is the only option. It ain't right, but there should be some more support for them so they can avoid that.

* * * * *

When I saw it was Judge McCrae again my heart sank. It was obvious what his decision would be. He never even took into account the fact that, with trials at Fulham and Millwall, I'd shown footballing promise, or how the shock of my parents returning to Jamaica affected me. McCrae threatened, 'If you come up before me again, I'll lose you in the system.' Charming. He thought he was giving me a chance with 'only' four years. They say time is a great healer, but I could never forgive Freddie for that.

Mum came to visit me when I was in Lavender Hill police station just after being sent down. I was only there because all the prisons were full. She cried, 'Son, why you doing this to me?' That hurt – it was the only time I ever cried.

Then, when I was sentenced, I was in Wandsworth for one day before going to Camp Hill on the Isle of Wight. It didn't sink in that I was going away for all that time until they slipped a note under my cell door saying where I was going the next day. Paul Speller's mum, Brenda, was surprised when she heard I'd gone to prison again. She thought I'd wasted my football talent. Brenda understood why Paul came to visit but didn't fully approve, feeling he was naïve. But Ray and I are godfathers to Paul's two kids so she must have seen some good in me.

When I got arrested Yankee moved out quick. Back in those days his brother and uncle both had reputations as bad boys, but my crew was coming up them times. His uncle with his feisty self ran up to my sister and said, 'Lucky he's in jail 'cos we would have killed him!' Yankee's brother sees me now all the time and always hails me, more out of fear though, than friendship. To be fair to him though, he had to defend his brother's honour.

Even though she never had much money, Val always came to visit me in all of the seven places I went to in total. It seemed like I went on tour in a big white bus. I've seen Freddie a couple of times since and just had to bite my tongue. I don't normally wish bad on people, but I wish that on him. Val sometimes sees Yankee in Croydon now and he gets off the bus quickly. Once I saw him when I had just got out of jail and he crossed the road so fast he nearly got run over.

* * * * *

The Isle of Wight must be the prison capital of the world. It has three prisons right beside each other.

There's the Category-A Parkhurst, which holds some of the worst criminals in Britain. I stayed there for the first week of my sentence. Then there's Albany opposite Parkhurst for Category-B inmates. And further up the hill is Camp Hill, a Category-C. It was opened about seventy years ago by Winston Churchill when he was Secretary of State. Camp Hill holds 580 prisoners in nine wings. It has a strong rehabilitation programme offering computer skills, tradesmen courses and further education classes. Thankfully, it had a great gym and football pitch so I had plenty of opportunities to stay fit and focused on preparing to do something worthwhile when I got out – becoming a footballer.

The day I was sentenced though, playing in the Premiership seemed about as likely as becoming President of the United States. It just weren't happening. I was banged up with Ambrose Mendy, the smooth-talking former manager of Nigel Benn, who had been at Camp Hill for a while after being convicted of fraud (though he'd later be acquitted). Mendy had all the patter and used to entertain people with his stories of mixing with the celebrities. Some were true but some were obviously porkies. He just didn't know when and how to stop lying. At least he did have a football connection, being Paul Ince's agent in the move from West Ham to Man United years earlier.

When I got to Camp Hill I put my name up to use the public phone. A bad boy inmate wanting to jump the queue threatened me. Expecting this skinny kid in glasses to be intimidated, he started doing fancy karate stances when I didn't back off. I grabbed him and knocked him to bits. But I broke my hand. When Paul Speller came to visit, he couldn't believe my hand was in a sling.

For most of my time at Camp Hill I shared a cell with Simpson 'Simmo' Sabaroche. A London-born Dominican, he was in for credit card fraud. Simmo, three inches taller and broader, effectively became my personal trainer. We hit it off straight away and would pump iron and train non-stop in our cell and the gym. As a youth, Simmo had played football at a high level and appreciated how good I was on the prison side.

Every Boxing Day Dale Young used to take Cowes Sports to play the Camp Hill prison team. I was outstanding. That day I played so well that Dale applied for me to get day release passes. They were in the semi-pro Wessex League. Dale was their player-manager, a former semi-pro defender. 'If I can get Jamie out, he'll be a revelation,' Dale told the governor. Obsessed with my future, having no access to outside vices, I was so fit and strong.

Initially though, Dale couldn't play me because I was still recovering from the broken hand. I couldn't wait for it to heal. The prison authorities didn't want to allow me out initially to play for Cowes Sports, fearing I might abscond. They only changed their minds when I'd come back on time after home leave.

After a lot of hassle, he got me out on contract. He would come and pick me up and sign me out at the gate. Cowes Sports' home ground was at the yachting club. They were still in the Hampshire League and wanted to be promoted to the Wessex League. I enjoyed the games, but the best bit was a couple of pints of Guinness afterwards. Dale made sure I had cheese and onion rolls, and lots of packets of chewing gum to mask the smell. The arrangement worked so well that I was even allowed to play in away games.

The first time I played away was in Petersfield. A warden came with me. The television programme GMTV heard about the story and interviewed me. We won and I scored – a blinding day. I scored a few, rarely with my head, but I enjoyed making them. The one time I scored with a header everyone made a fuss. Most of the teams were wary of me because of my reputation.

As I continued to play for Cowes Sports the media got really interested. The local Meridian TV did an interview and the local papers were regularly making me Man of the Match. Camp Hill's management was very proud of me as it gave the prison excellent publicity for its programme of rehabilitating inmates. Simmo and me were getting a few perks. No one seemed to resent it because we lifted spirits in the prison. Practically every night we trained in our cell – bunny hops, press-ups, sit-ups, pools of sweat every time. We'd shower, then play dominoes or draughts, maybe read the papers or chat. We'd battle to see who was fitter, stronger or faster. Six years younger, I'd usually win and gloat. It was all in good humour, even the Jamaica-big-island-Dominica-small-island banter helped keep us going. I was a Yardie Bum, he was a Dominican Fool.

Camp Hill is a typical prison with four or five landings, narrow balconies and iron cell doors with peepholes for the screws to look into. Our cell had bunk beds not big enough for grown men. We were given two cotton sheets. One, you lay on the bed and the other, you put over you to protect yourself from the coarse blanket, which was unbelievably itchy. If you didn't have eczema, those blankets would have given it to you. We felt blessed because we had a toilet cubicle so didn't have to do it into a bucket in front of each other and slop out, unlike some other unlucky bastards. Walls were creamy-yellow. We were issued with bog-standard prison clothes of blue, denim jeans, a couple of T-shirts and a couple of blue shirts.

We built ourselves up so much that when we were released some people didn't recognise us. We were the wing 'daddies'. Everyone came to us with tobacco, which is prison currency. Double bubble, one packet of biscuits, or whatever, in exchange for two. We were rich: it worked nicely, we had proper charisma. Simmo even says that sharing the cell with me helped make his sentence almost enjoyable. 'Doing bird with you didn't affect me like prison should have,' Simmo says. 'It made it go so fast. I'd done bird before and hated it. Soul destroying, disheartening, but this time it was okay.'

An ex-grammar schoolboy, Simmo became the prison reporter and even taped an interview with me. He transcribed it all, convinced I was going to make it as a pro. We were not just cellmates, but soulmates, too. Simmo followed my career when I got out and has nuff shirts from me.

Dale was so impressed with my game that he contacted Southampton and insisted they come and watch me. They watched a number of times and Dale felt they were impressed, but shied away because of my image. He invited Portsmouth to send scouts, too, and although they came, they weren't impressed enough. Dale thought I could do a Lee Bradbury. He was in the army playing for an amateur side, Dale tipped them off and he ended up at Portsmouth.

Dale felt I would fit in partly because I was fitter than most of the Cowes Sports players. Being banged up 24-7 and not getting a chance to party plus training every day meant I was bound to be very fit. Cowes Sports only trained once a week, but my energy levels were tremendous. Dale liked my ball control. Sure, I had my off days but most of the time I was the main difference between the sides. It also helped my temperament because part of the prison contract was not to get into trouble on the pitch. The whole time, over one and a half seasons, I was never booked.

One press cutting I'm particularly proud of reads: 'Most of the excitement for Cowes came in the form of James Lawrence, who had another outstanding match as he embarrassed the Horndean rearguard. Lawrence was in exhilarating form and the mainlanders frequently resorted to unfair tactics to stop him.'

I was nervous the first few times but the players made me feel welcome. They recognised me from the Boxing Day match – not hard with a pineapple barnet! My time with Cowes Sport was so successful that other inmates wanted the special treatment. But they changed the prison rules after that, otherwise it would have been chaos. I effectively changed the rules. The only screw not pleased for me was Mr Holt. He once tried to deny me home leave when I came back one day after the time he thought I should have returned. He didn't realise that I'd played for the prison on the Saturday and was entitled to the extra day.

'You're going to get nicked,' Holt sneered. 'I don't think so,' I said. The Governor came on the wing. I told him and he smiled. 'Don't worry about that, Jamie. I'll sort it out.' Holt was furious. He thought every prisoner should suffer, have no privileges and be treated like shit. That's long – what a horrible piece of work.

In all my prison experiences the best warden was Eddie Walder, one of the senior staff who managed the prison team. Top man. I'm still in touch with him all these years later. He believed in me so much that, when Dale Young approached him, Eddie pulled some strings to allow me to play for Cowes Sports. He was under no obligation to help me, but he admired how determined I was and the clincher was that I never, ever retaliated when fouled. The discipline I'd learnt as a kid with Pete Rhodes was paying off. 'You'll be an excellent ambassador for the prison,' Eddie said and I didn't let him down.

Eddie thought that with a little more coaching from him, he could have made me a better goal scorer. There was one incident that could have worked against me, though, the time the inmates played against the staff. When I challenged a warden, even though it felt like only a nudge, he fell awkwardly and broke his arm. There was no malice. I was so apologetic. Everyone appreciated that. And it impressed Eddie enough to ensure I got a chance with Cowes Sports. He even told the local paper: 'If Saints want to take James for a week's trial, that would not prove difficult. I have cleared it with the Governor at Camp Hill, and James could live near The Dell, if need be.'

Southampton came so often to see me that everyone thought it was inevitable and it gave me an extra incentive to play well. Watford and Portsmouth kept coming, too. It was exciting and nerve-wracking at the same time, wondering whether any of them would give me a chance. In the end, after all that, they didn't bother.

Out on home leave, I played in a charity match in east London with my mate, Winston Clarke. Years later, he told me: 'You were quicker than anyone else and hit the ball so hard when scoring into the top corner I thought, "Wow, who's that?"' Winston didn't know me, but on that one showing he was convinced I could be a full-time pro.

With my increasing media coverage, the Prison Service was holding me up as a shining example of the good things jail can do for those who really want to reform. It was going so well. Others were being released to do all sorts of things in the arts, music, sport, workplace and academia. But it all came to a sudden halt when Michael Howard, Home Secretary at the time, stopped it after a prisoner who was out on special permission absconded and killed someone. There had been a lot of opposition to us having what the media termed as 'jollies' and this was a convenient reason for Howard to stop it. The FA pleaded with him to change his mind, but Howard weren't having it.

For years after that, Eddie Walder followed my progress, sticking up press clippings on the prison notice board. 'Jamie, you inspired a whole generation of kids, who wanted to better themselves,' he told me. 'Many wanted to do the same as you, but didn't have the ability. But at least you got them believing in themselves. A couple of players, like Ricky Otto, had more ability than you. He made it, but didn't last. Some of the others were too horrible to deserve success. But you were different and I'm really, really proud of you.'

Nice words, but along with resuming my football career, after all those months banged up, there was another sort of banging I wanted to do: sex, and plenty of it. Before I met Rowena, my partner and mother of our daughter Tiagh, one girl in my life was never enough. It must be the testosterone coursing through my veins. Beautiful women are one of life's great pleasures and I could never resist a pretty face and a nice figure. My record for sex with different girls in one day is three. I used to plan meeting them like a military operation. A couple of times I got close to doing four in twenty-four hours, but things never quite worked out.

My insecurity with girls stems from being let down a couple of times as a teenager. I may have fucked one of Kerrie's cousins but Kerrie still hurt me, just like Tasha. That made me not trust women too much. After just a couple of months Tasha cheated on me when I was in jail. I suppose she was a young woman with her own needs, but I thought she was the love of my life. I was in a cell hearing all this shit when I decided I wouldn't allow a woman to hurt me again. After her, I was immune to emotional hurt. I did all the hiring and firing after that.

When I came out of prison the girls loved the dreadlocks, especially the way I tied them up. When I checked a girl in a Leicester club I took her back to a hotel and eventually ended up getting creative with some bottles. Wild! I asked a mate if he wanted to fuck her after I was done but he said, 'I'm not going after you. What's the point with a package like yours?' She was still there in the morning, sleeping. I sneaked out with my things to move into digs – I can't be in no small talk. Left her £10 to get a cab home...

Chapter 6

SPIV MENTALITY

By the time I left Camp Hill in April 1993 I'd become blasé about the media coverage. The press and cameras were coming regular. I was in the newspapers all the time and became a celebrity on the island. I'd been playing every week, local papers loved me and I was a proper celeb. The prison gave me parole knowing it was football's pre-season and on 13 July 1993 I was released. I knew I had a trial lined up with Southend United. Ambrose Mendy lined it up for me. The day before I was released he phoned me in Camp Hill to tell me. It's funny, all the time I was playing inside and getting the publicity I'd never heard from him, but just when I was about to be released, that's when he crawled out of the woodwork...

Coming out of prison at twenty-three I didn't expect to reap the benefits for years to come. On leaving

Camp Hill my constant worry was what was I going to do next – more crime? I'd trained hard because there might be a chance in football. Whatever prison I was sent to they said I should be a pro. Even the screws agreed. So I kept my head down. If anyone started a beef with me, I'd dealt with it. A football career was the only legit option and this time I wouldn't waste any time or energy on negative things.

My first hairstyle was the pineapple. It was in jail, first at Feltham, then Brixton, and then Dover. Jazzie B was around them times and the funki-dread style was the lick. I had nuff time to twist up my head. Man used to have patterns on their heads, all kinds of intricate styles. The barber in each prison had no idea of how to do a fade – they were like sheep shearers! I just started locksing up on top to give it a style. Nuff man in prison was locksing up, so I got into it, too. When girls came to visit, I felt like a don 'cos I was different to the shaven-headed, sweet-boy style. In youth centres screws are relaxed about your hair, but in detention centres you've got the sergeant major shit. If I wanted to shave my hair off, I'd have to make an application to the governor, for example. I suppose it was in case you escaped. They always wanted you to look like your photos. Being banged up isn't nice. My message to anyone thinking that it's worth taking the risk should consider that the little things you take for granted are suddenly not there anymore, simple things like going to the fridge to get a snack. You have to be strong, but in a way it made me a better person because I realised how simple things should be appreciated. Boy, was I looking forward to doing ordinary things.

With all the media attention the day I got out, I felt like a film star. I got a lift from Dale Young from the prison to the ferry in a minibus. They kicked me out with £60 and I had to make it stretch. With that sort of start after nearly two years of incarceration, how the hell is anybody supposed to go straight? As soon as I got to London I dropped off my things at my bredren Donny's flat in Hammersmith. I went to Ambrose Mendy's office in Stratford, east London and he gave me £200 to keep me going. That was a nice gesture but he also wanted me to sign a contract. Just like that – no lawyer, advisor or even friend for guidance. Of course, it wasn't a normal contract. He wanted to take a big percentage of my signing-on fee and a large cut of my wages. It's normal for an agent to earn off you, but not what he wanted. I'd heard rumours about the way he operated. I headed to Val's and then went on the hunt to find girls. There was a lot of sexual tension to release. I was able to kill two birds with one stone because I had to see Sherry (I'd met her on home leave) in nearby Leyton.

On my second sentence I made the decision not to get properly involved with girls because I'd been hurt by Tasha on my first sentence. She did my head in. To get me through Camp Hill, all I did was write to some chicks and have some sex talk. I was writing to loads of different girls. Jail is hard enough without your girl fucking with your head. Not being focused on one chick made it so much easier without the added pressure of wondering what your partner was doing whilst you're banged up. Nuff man has gone mad and even had nervous breakdowns whilst doing their bird because their imaginations run wild about what their missus is up to out there, especially the ones with kids. It's not like they can just forget about their partner and decide to move on when released. At least I wasn't a father yet so there wasn't that complication. Some have even got suicidal... My first night out and I spent it with Sherry – heaven! There was a lot of sexual frustration waiting to be released.

* * * * *

Training with Southend United the next day, I didn't have time to settle in. Bare excitement is what I craved after being released. There was a lot of catching up to do. Barry Fry was the manager. He is one of those great characters football needs to keep it exciting, a Cockney wheeler-dealer always looking for a bargain he can sell on. Maybe that's why he gave me a trial when very few others were prepared to.

There were some good, seasoned pros at Southend, like Chris Powell, Andy Clarke, Ricky Otto (who had also just come out of jail) and Andy Ansah. Ricky

Otto gave me some sound advice. He was perfectly placed as he had been in the same prison, same wing and had done the same sentence for the same offence. Ricky took me under his wing and I was very grateful for that.

Training at Southend for a month was an eye-opener. I felt I didn't do myself justice, partly because I thought I was already fit but soon realised that the pros were fitter. The first session we went long-distance running on the beach. I woke up the next morning and I ached so much I knew I was in trouble. Ambrose Mendy's son Wesley was trying to get in at Southend, too. I felt he was competing against me, mainly because his dad was paying attention to me.

When you come out of jail, your confidence takes a huge knock. I didn't understand the culture of banter at Southend and thought it was personal. I felt they were picking on me and used to think, 'Tell me a little bit more and if you carry on I'll have to fist you up.' But at the same time I realised that I'd just got released and had to hold it down. At least I was seeing a lot of girls, just casual, to help enjoy my newfound liberty.

Catching up with all the ladies I'd been dreaming of was as big a priority as a football career. I was rampant. Did the business with Francesca and Susan on the same day. I had a mate called Lee Cooper (real name!) He let us get down in his flat in Brixton. Francesca came back to Dunston. All the man was there so I just took her behind a van and had my wicked way. She was game as. It was just what I needed at the time. After that I was still feeling tusky so I got a blow-job off Francesca in another girl's flat. I also had my girlfriend's cousin in Daley Thompson Way. It was truly a gold medal performance. Shelly was coming on to me. I said to her, 'See you outside in five minutes.' I took her over my girlfriend's car. She found out and told her cousin – not me – to fuck off! Maybe she was making a big concession for me being away for so long without any poom. But it had to be done...

After a month, Fry told Ambrose, 'We haven't got anything here for Jamie.' To build up my fitness levels, Ambrose got me training at a boxing gym in east London two or three times a week. I was running, too. But after a while he admitted he couldn't get me a trial so he brought in Barry Silkman. He'd been a pro at a lot of clubs in the seventies and eighties, including Crystal Palace and Manchester City. Silky had a lot of contacts and he could open a few more doors than Ambrose.

In July 1993 I met Silky in the Swallow Hotel in Waltham Abbey. I thought I'd arrived. After years in prison it seemed like a palace. I'd heard so much about the salmon on the hotel menu and ordered it, then immediately regretted it. It looked raw, smelt foul and came with a little bit of lettuce. To be polite, I had to force it down.

Through Silky, I met Clive Berlin, who fixed me up

with a reserve match for Millwall at West Ham's training ground. We drew 1-1 and I set up the goal. I did some good things but I wasn't at my best. Mick McCarthy was managing Millwall those days and I went to train for a month. He was alright. I played two reserve games. The first was at The New Den (can't remember who we were playing). The second was away to Watford. I ripped up the left back, Jason Drysdale, who was supposed to be shit-hot. Terrorised him. Kevin Keegan later bought him for £425,000 at Newcastle so he couldn't have been a mug.

Silky was convinced I could make it even though my past and age were against me. Mick McCarthy offered me a contract of £200 a week. Not much, but I was considering it because there were few options. But when Millwall wanted to put me in digs with kids because of my recent past there was no way. I'd just come out of prison and they wanted to put me back in. Silky couldn't believe they hadn't offered me a decent deal. He was touting my name around, but my past was putting them off.

Silky got me in at Wimbledon. Joe Kinnear was the manager. The Crazy Gang with Fash, Vinny & Co was still going strong. I played in a reserve game against Crystal Palace at Plough Lane. It was a tiny, scruffy ground, but the pitch was perfect. After prison pitches, Hackney Marshes and Purley Way, it was like Wembley to me. They offered me £250 a week, but still it wasn't enough to live on in London. I was getting desperate. The lure of crime was still there, but then a breakthrough...

By mid-October, Silky had convinced his mate, Ian Atkins (assistant manager at Sunderland at the time) to sign me. 'This kid is twenty-three, inexperienced, not fit and raw, but I'm absolutely convinced he's good enough to make it,' he told a reluctant Atkins. 'It will also do him good to get away from the bad influences in London.' Atkins eventually agreed to a trial. Talk about different culture – everything was totally different from London. He put me up in a hotel in Washington, at the Queen Victoria. At the time I thought it was plush, but I've experienced much better since. Their accents were funny; I couldn't understand them.

I played in a game on the following Thursday and I was much fitter than at Millwall. Their leftback was Kevin Sharpe and I ripped him to shreds. Next day Terry Butcher said the most magical words, 'Son, you excite me – I want to sign you.' I was excited, but it was tinged with the thought that Up North is kinda far and I'd be 300 miles from my boys. The following Tuesday at Leicester I had to play again. We drew 1-1. I played alright and I was on the team bus for the first time with all my gear from London. They didn't really know how to take me.

I signed on the Friday and made my debut on the Sunday against Middlesbrough away at Ayresome Park. It was a local derby. I was in dreamland. One minute I was in jail eating porridge, the next I was playing for Sunderland, live on Sky in front of a packed stadium. Inmate to team mate, prisoner to principal, low life to high life. Life can throw up some crazy situations and you couldn't make up a bigger contrast. The rush was intoxicating.

People talk about crime not paying. Well, it did alright for me. If I'd never gone to jail I don't think I would have made it. Doing bird gave me the chance to concentrate on the things that are important to me, to refocus and build myself up. As they say, good things come from bad situations. I would love to tell all the youths out there who are going through bad times and think that their lives are over: don't despair: you can turn your life around. As long as the desire and ambition is there, you can do it. I'm a prime example. It doesn't necessarily have to be football or sport – there are many opportunities in prison now to get proper rehabilitation. Reds, one of my bredrens I was in Dover with, is now a successful property developer, Simmo is a businessman, Luton is doing well. Nuff others have made good and are responsible family men, who have distanced themselves from all that badness.

We lost 4-1 and I came on just for a run out for the last twenty minutes when the game was already lost. But it was still a buzz. While I was warming up, they played 'Jailhouse Rock' on the tannoy. I liked the humour, but some of the Middlesbrough fans gave me stick. When I made my debut I wasn't nervous. How could it be intimidating after being in front of a judge who's taken away my liberty?

* * * * *

Sunderland was cool once I settled there. It helped that the girls up there loved me. Everywhere I went they'd ask to feel my hair and, of course, I took advantage. Everyone was going to get it. The best thing that happened socially was when David Rush came back from a loan spell at Peterborough. I really clicked with Rushie, a centre-forward, born and bred in Sunderland and a local hero. His popularity was sealed when he scored the winning goal in the FA Cup quarter final against Chelsea. He liked the ladies, was down to earth and could drink like a fish so we had a lot in common. He was wild and took me everywhere. We were like Bonnie and Clyde, took no prisoners. Wicked times.

On the Tuesday after the Middlesbrough game, Martin Smith and me made our debuts. He scored a goal in our 2-0 win and I played well, but was so exhausted. Butcher took me off after eighty-one minutes. That standing ovation was one of the best experiences I've ever had, a wicked relief after all the years of incarceration and uncertainty. In the local paper I was quoted as saying, 'That was the best day of my life. It was just fantastic. Everything has happened so quickly and I'm still trying to take it all in.' But my outstanding memory of the game was the reception I got from the supporters. They were superb and when they chanted my name, I felt ten feet tall.

The fans really gave me the Roker Roar. It was tremendous. The whole game was magic. After the dark days in prison, I couldn't see how my life was going to turn out. Terry Butcher said, 'Jamie is the talk of the team. There was a buzz about the place when he got the ball. He could prove to be a gem.' *The Sun*, typically, couldn't resist the prison angle: 'James Lawrence was given a four-year jail sentence for robbery with violence – now he has been given the licence to go out and mug First Division defences.'

To prove I wasn't getting carried away, I told the press: 'I can do a lot better than that. I'm working on my fitness and once that comes right, I'll be a yard faster. That will help me get past defenders more easily. But I'm not taking anything for granted as far as Saturday is concerned. I'd love to be in the side, but I realise there are quite a few players who were not available at Luton, who should be ready by then.'

We went to Julie's nightclub in Newcastle that night – Rush, Don Goodman, Kevin Ball, Derek Ferguson, Gary Bennett, and a few others. I felt I'd earned their respect. That night was the first time I met Andy Cole, who was already a legend at Newcastle. He came over and chatted, and made me feel welcome even though we were with a rival team. We were at the foot of the

First Division and Newcastle was flying. But it didn't matter to me. Anything legit, earning decent money, was better than jail.

I must say a big thank you to Terry Butcher for giving me the chance. I was so sure that my career would eventually take off that I was reported saying to the local paper: 'Now all that prison stuff is behind me, I hope to use the money I earn at Sunderland to pay for my parents to return and live in England.' That's how big a wrench their leaving was on me.

But Sunderland was struggling. Soon after, Butcher got sacked and the new manager, Mick Buxton, was a sergeant-major type. It came as no surprise when he didn't want me. Butcher getting sacked was a big blow. To me, he had an understanding of players that Buxton could never match. Talk about contrast of football backgrounds; Butcher had played at the top level for Ipswich, Rangers and Sunderland, won nuff cups and championships. He'd played seventy-seven times for England under some of the shrewdest managers in the British game. There was absolutely nothing he hadn't done as a player that didn't deserve maximum respect. But as for Buxton... His only credential was managing Scunthorpe for four years with moderate success. When, after winning only twenty-five games out of seventy-six, Sunderland sacked Buxton and he went back to Scunthorpe – probably the only team willing to give him another chance. No wonder we didn't get on!

Terry Butcher knew how to relate to players, and how to get the best out of players with less talent than himself without talking down to them. That's why he'll always be successful as a manager. He's at Motherwell in the Scottish Premier at the time of writing and doing well with limited resources. If I had a problem, Terry would sit me down and discuss it, work things out man to man. But Mick Buxton, he'd just tell you to get on with it. As soon as he took charge, I knew that was the beginning of the end...

I got an ankle injury playing in a reserve game in December 1993 and was out for three or four weeks and Buxton didn't pick me again. He wore a flat cap and I swear he thought anyone from outside the county was a foreigner. So imagine what he thought of me with my highlighted pineapple, designer clothes, tattoos and gold tooth.

* * * * *

At least the partying got better with David Rush. After training we'd go straight out and party, maybe until six-thirty or seven the next morning before snatching two or three hours' sleep and going into training again. Rush was the local idol there. He had played in the FA Cup final for Sunderland in 1992 against Liverpool.

Don Goodman reckons Sunderland didn't know how to handle me. 'They'd never seen anything like you,' he said. 'Your pineapple got you noticed and you certainly weren't a shy lad. You really did enjoy going out with Rushie, didn't you? Rushie couldn't sustain it after a while. It didn't affect your game, though. You did ever so well at adapting to Division One football.'

Goodman was surprised at the heaviness of the weights I used to work out. He said: 'I can't believe how strong you was.' This influenced some of the lads, who realised how hard it was to knock me off the ball. I didn't tire so much towards the end of a game so they started working out with weights, too. Goodman reckons I was ahead of my time with my weights programme – now it's the routine at all clubs.

To ease the boredom when I had to be low-key, snooker was a great time killer. James Hunter, the local football writer, played some enjoyable frames with me. He couldn't believe my intensity to win and remembers a time when Kerrie, my girlfriend at the time, came up from London and I kept her there for hours playing snooker with James. At least she got well fed with plenty of sandwiches.

I was young, had nuff energy and a lot of partying to catch up on, so it comes as no surprise that I really didn't get on with Buxton, nor his assistant, Trevor Hartley, who was always on my case. I don't know if it was his way of trying to get the best out of me, but it didn't work. At training one day Hartley slapped me round my head; clapped me real hard, can't remember what for. I looked at him and in my mind I was begging for him to do it again. My parents had believed in corporal punishment, but they'd never hit me like that. I wanted to lift Hartley up, but knew it would have been the end of my career before it even started. He was very lucky I didn't lose it.

There was a brief spell when things looked up. Making an impression in the reserves, I got an unexpected call-up to the first-team squad. It caught me on the hop. I'd turned up for training on Friday with an overnight bag intending to catch the train back to London to see Kerrie. Buxton took me to one side and told me I was going on the coach to the Midlands for the West Brom game. I thought I was just going for the ride until I walked into the visitors' dressing room at the Hawthorns. I couldn't believe it when I saw my shirt hanging on the peg. It was a lovely surprise. The fact that I was only a substitute and didn't even get on the pitch didn't really matter: I felt Buxton was going to give me a proper chance. But it was too good to be true. A month later I was out, having played only five games in six months.

My time at Sunderland may have been brief but I evidently made an impression because Martin McFadden, the editor of their fanzine, *A Love Supreme*, remembers me well – but not necessarily for my football. 'When you first came to Sunderland my first impression was your crazy haircut,' he said. 'We were also curious because we knew of your past.'

McFadden featured me in his fanzine's 'Jailbird XI' and 'Bad Hair XI'. The next time he saw me play was for Bradford and he was amazed by my improvement. I was more hardworking then, having knuckled down. I'm glad I proved to him and the Sunderland fans that I was capable of proving myself as a pro. Football is the biggest thing in Sunderland. Anyone who plays for them is immediately a celebrity and although I didn't last long there, I'm glad I made an impression. McFadden puts me in the same category as Robin Friday, who played for Reading in the seventies. Although a brilliant striker, he lived like a rock star, was in and out of prison, had a drug and alcohol problem and died at thirty-eight. I'm wild, but not that crazy.

The last time I played for Sunderland was in February 1994 when I was on the subs bench away to West Brom. I was on my way out after only six months and five games and this time I prayed I was going to a club where the manager really appreciated me.

Chapter 7

BUTCHER'S BEST

Sunderland moved me out of the hotel and into a bed and breakfast on the seafront. It was very cold up there, freezing most of the time. In training we were only allowed to wear the waterproof wet top, plus shorts. It was bitterly cold, but I was tough. I used to bring girls back to my place, but the couple who ran the b&b I was staying in didn't really like it.

I had my twenty-fourth birthday in March 1994 just before I left Sunderland. My girlfriend, Kerrie, brought up a cake in the shape of a football – nice gesture. She was always very thoughtful, but the relationship couldn't last, partly because of the distance and also because I would outgrow her.

I hadn't been on much money at Sunderland – £300 a week and Butcher had been signing off all my bills in the hotel. I got a £10,000 signing-on fee at

Sunderland, which was very nice compared to my prison wages of a few quid. After tax it was just over six grand, a fortune for me. That money was the green light for me to party and shop – all the latest designer gear. Needless to say, it went very quickly, quick as a fuck. Armani was the lick then. Jeans cost about £120 and shirts were £140. Timberlands, too. Anything good, I was buying it. That dough went rapid. Buxton called me into his office, where he had the hotel receipts and invoices in front of him. He said he wasn't paying the bills anymore, especially the phone bills which amounted to thousands. Being so far away from my friends and family in London, I used to be on the phone for hours. Buxton started docking my money to pay the bills.

The final straw came that Christmas. My nephew, Ray, was seriously ill and I asked for a few days off to visit him. Buxton told me I could have only one day off, which was ridiculous because it's a full day's journey to get to London. But I was only one of a few people who could help Ray and really needed to go down there. I knew I wasn't trying to have Buxton's pants off as this was a genuine crisis and so I ended up staying ten days to make sure Ray was well, then went back to take my punishment. Buxton fined me a week's wages. He looked like he enjoyed annoying people, reminded me of a screw.

In the New Year I was injured and got very low. I was close to Rushie and a few team-mates. Kerrie worked in a solicitor's office, which is ironic – she came into my life too late to help. She and Paul Speller used to come up on a coach to keep me company in the hotel. It took seven hours, sometimes longer, and I'll always be grateful to them for that. With Rushie we had a lot of fun with girls. I couldn't behave myself with so much temptation around. It was like paradise. As soon as we went out to a club, the DJ would announce we were there and the girls would just log on. There was no hostility from the guys because we were with their beloved club. They were terrific, especially as they had heard my story and a lot of them had been through that kind of experience.

* * * * *

Living in Sunderland was great, but as Mick Buxton didn't want me I was desperate to move on. Thankfully, Ian Atkins signed me for £20,000 at Doncaster Rovers on 17 March 1994. What a relief! He'd moved on from Sunderland. Atkins was good to me and treated me properly. He saw my potential and wanted to nurture it.

I made my debut away two days later to Wycombe Wanderers as a sub with twenty minutes to go. Martin O'Neill was making his way as manager at Wycombe Wanderers then and his great motivational skills were beginning to show. We were poor and lost 3-0. The next game was Wigan away and we drew 0-0. But homesickness for London was still strong. Disillusioned, I went missing for the next game. I was desperate to spend some time with Kerrie and my family – it seemed crazy that I hardly saw them when I was now a free man, and after two years of prison life I just wanted to catch up with them. Besides, it was exceptionally cold up there! When I returned to Doncaster, they were annoyed, but because my money was so poor (a couple of hundred basic), they didn't fine me. Their brand of football didn't suit me either. Ian Atkins liked to lump it to the corners and we didn't play much football. As a winger I wasn't getting much action. Anyway, I wasn't properly fit and also my confidence had taken a battering from Buxton and Hartley.

We played Darlington away and from a right cross I got ahead of my marker to score with a diving header – my first goal in professional football. It was not just a nice feeling scoring for the first time: more importantly, I felt I earned the team's respect. We lost 3-1 at Colchester and won 1-0 at Hereford to close the season in the Third Divison in fifthteenth place at the end of May 1994. Only 1,603 people were at Hereford's ground that day. It definitely wasn't Old Trafford.

The team were a great bunch. Russ Wilcox, the captain, was one of the best defenders in the lower leagues. He deserved a chance at a higher level but because he lacked a bit of pace, he didn't get it – he more than made up for that by how well he read the game. Kevin Hulme was another mad one, but also a one hundred per cent honest midfielder. 'Bomber' Jones was our centre-forward. I see him in Marbella most summers. He was a good scorer. Then there was a Geordie called David Roche. I knew him from my Sunderland days. Good player, but he went the wrong way. He allegedly got shot and stabbed someone, and went to prison. One of my team-mates – let's call him Crappy - was the funniest man ever, but dirty. His party piece was to shit in the communal bath – nasty! He would get in and you would just see a steaming turd coming to the top of the bath. Whenever Crappy approached, I would get out. Of the others, Paul Marquis – who came later – and Sam Kitchen were decent men, on and off the pitch.

When I think about it, as a professional footballer, at times I was a disgrace. I was living in a house with another player (Lee Luscombe) and we were partying 24-7. It got so bad that I once puked up on the bus going to a game. Atkins didn't know, but he would have slung me off. The night before the game I had been out all night. I went out, intending to stay for half an hour, but it ended up being an all-nighter.

But I wasn't an exception: the whole team was off-key like that. It was full of mad men. Besides David Roche and the captain, Russ Wilcox big characters that came later and made my stay at Belle Vue so enjoyable included Gary Brabin, Warren Hackett, Mick Norbury, Ryan Kirby, Stephen Gallam, James

O'Meara, O'Neill Donaldson, Sean Parrish and Paul Marcus. They were all like me. We went out together mainly because few of them had serious girlfriends. Young boys having fun. Our facilities were crap. We even had to wash our own kit, like a Sunday League pub side, but the laughs and sense of unity kept us going. Washing your own tatty training kit and leaving it in the boiler room to dry to a crisp was one of the reasons why we called ourselves Rag-Arse Rovers. But at least the team spirit was solid.

* * * * *

That first season wasn't very memorable but we really did well in the next year, moving up from fifteenth to ninth in the division. The team spirit was brilliant. We had a mad chairman, too: Ken Richardson. When he took over the club, he pumped a lot of his own money into it, but when things didn't go well he hatched a bizarre plan.

In 1999 Richardson was charged and convicted of trying to burn down the Doncaster ground in 1995 for the insurance money. He was convicted of conspiracy to commit arson and jailed for four years. Apparently, he offered £10,000 to a former SAS soldier to start the fire at the club's ground. It caused about £100,000 of damage. Richardson didn't just want the insurance money – he was trying to force Rovers to move to a new stadium. It was alleged that the plan failed when Alan Kristiansen, who was hired to start the fire, left his mobile at the scene and a message on Richardson's answering machine saying, 'The job's been done.' That's the kind of chairman we had. He used to get players to sign and promised them a bung so that we wouldn't have to declare it and pay tax. But he wouldn't pay it straight away and if you weren't playing well, you wouldn't get your money. It happened to me: I didn't get my £2,000.

There was an Icelandic centre-forward, Gunner Torfason, who at first was scoring regularly and even got a sponsored car included in his contract. But then his form dipped. Ken Richardson wanted his car back, so one day we were all training together and we saw the physio jump in the car and drive away in it. When Torfason got back to the changing room there was a black bag filled with all his possessions. Richardson paid him off and we never saw him again.

The pull of London in the early days was so strong that I'd overstay my time down there and just go missing. Atkins was losing his patience. Once he phoned Silky and said, 'That's it, I've had enough – I don't want him back.' Not knowing where the hell I was, Silky made an excuse that I had a lot of personal problems to sort out. I phoned Silky and told him that two girls I was seeing had met and fought, and I just didn't have my mind on football. Silky phoned Atkins and pleaded for another favour because of the woman trouble. Reluctantly, Atkins gave me a final chance: 'Fine, as long as he's Man of the Match!'

I returned, had a blinder, we won and I totally redeemed myself. Under pressure to keep his job, Atkins said, 'Jamie, you can go missing every week if you like.' But it didn't save him and he got sacked that first summer. I felt he didn't have enough time to settle. Once Richardson loses patience with you, you're out.

Sammy Chung and his assistant George Smith took over. I arrived a week late for pre-season training, mainly because I had nowhere to stay. Chung didn't fine me. On that money it would have been like cutting my legs off. Someone I shared my house with moved to another club and took all my clothes with him to the Isle of Man. We were the same size and he decided that my designer garms were worth thieving. He even took my shoes. Them times mobiles were scarce and I couldn't contact him. George Smith was like a sergeant major too, but he was like that to everybody. The new regime quickly took notice of me because, in a pre-season friendly, I had a brilliant game. The next day Chung called me into his office. 'How far do you want to go?' he asked. 'As far as I can,' I replied. 'Well, I think you can play for England. Every time you get the ball I want you to dribble. You've got the talent to go all the way. The fact that every time you get kicked, you still go back for more impresses me, too.' That gave me a lot of confidence.

Chung and Smith were a Godsend. I needed someone to believe one hundred per cent in me and they certainly did. I think if we had kept that team together, we would have been promoted. All footballers have egos: that's obvious. But our egos are very fragile, too. It only takes a small amount of criticism from the gaffer, say, or the fans, media, directors, whatever, and it can crush a player, no matter how good he is. Even seasoned internationals can be hurt, no matter how brilliant they are and how much they've achieved. That's the nature of the industry. If an office worker gets pulled up for shoddy work, there is no big ripple effect like in football where, if you're not performing, a whole ground can be on your case. You get nervous, frightened of the ball even. Confidence drained, you dread receiving anything less than a perfect pass in case you fuck things up. It's even worse when your team-mates lose confidence in you: that's when you know you should either move on, or get the hell out of football. I was never that low, but I've seen players fall apart through lack of confidence.

To have a manager and coach believing in you is a big part of the psychology of football. Fuck what anybody else thinks, if they love you chances are you'll overcome problems. That's why I had no respect for Mick Buxton and so much love for Terry Butcher. Buxton knew my circumstances, but made no allowances. Funny, in a way he made me a better player 'cos I was even more determined to prove him wrong.

*****

Desperate for somewhere to stay, I rang the club and they fixed me up in a room living with an old man in his bungalow. He had no interest in football and just wanted a tenant. People think everything about football is glamorous. Believe me, at that level it's anything but. At least something good came out of that experience because I had few distractions. I trained really hard and just went home to sleep after eating a takeaway. Proper grafting. Living with the old man I couldn't bring girls back. I had to resort to using a girl's car, a tiny Fiat 126. Natalie was tall and the space was small, so it wasn't easy to grind a girl in there. But she kept me going (I was splitting up with Kerrie at the time).

My wages were £350 a week, plus £50 an appearance. I was motivated by the signing-on fee and becoming a better player. It wasn't all rosy, but I had to persevere. I kept in touch with my people in London and used to go home after a Saturday match. At that time I used to look at the fixtures and pray for an away match in the South. Barnet is the only suitable club I can remember we played. Anywhere near to London was a Godsend!

I moved out of the old man's house and in with a

couple and a team-mate, Ryan Kirby. Living in digs with a middle-aged couple was stifling. They definitely didn't approve when I once took a girlfriend back there: they couldn't get rid of us fast enough. That's when we decided to rent a house together with O'Neill Donaldson. We were having a great time but then Ryan's girlfriend decided to live with us so we had to calm down a bit. Still great times. We even hired a huge sound system for a party for this little terraced house. My mates came up from London and had a fantastic time. The neighbours weren't too happy but we didn't do any harm. Once his girlfriend saw what we were going on with, she grounded Ryan. We were having a mad time and she put a stop to him joining us. She was far too possessive – he got rid of her that season.

Ryan was one of my best friends at Doncaster, partly because he was a Londoner, too. He was a bit younger (twenty) when he arrived from Arsenal. We got on well from the off. They thought I was crazy because I was always on the go. Ryan remembers how I always seemed to be the first one up ironing to music. He was used to going home after training, but started dressing smarter because after training we would always go out. Dean Williams, a keeper, used to pick us up for training, which was very convenient because we could go drinking after or shopping in Sheffield or Leeds. Sometimes it was snooker, or the pub, or both. We were on it 24-7.

I played wicked for Doncaster that season. Chung used to say to get the ball to Jamie. I played right wing, right midfield and centre-forward a few times. I didn't score many, about three, but I used to terrorise the opposition. They couldn't hold me. When I left, we were third in the table.

* * * * *

One of my best mates from Doncaster was Gary Brabin, who was a central midfielder. I had my pineapple haircut them times, so they called me 'Shabba' after Shabba Ranks, the dancehall star. Gary always had faith in me because he said he could see how honest and hardworking I was on the pitch. He truly believed I could go on to better things and even though I did play at a much higher level than Third Division, he feels I could have done even better.

One mad weekend we had been drinking two days solid and were on our way to training from a party at nine in the morning. I asked Gary to pull up at a shop. He thought it was to get a paper and some snacks, and couldn't believe it when I got in with an eight-pack of Guinness. The mere smell of drink made him nauseous, but I was fine.

Warren Hackett was a centre-half in that Doncaster side. A Londoner too, we used to organise travelling between ourselves as half the team was from the South. It made for a tight unit. Warren was amazed at my libido. He can't forget the time a group of us were walking through Doncaster town centre to a pub and some girls recognised us. I disappeared with one of them and turned up in the pub half an hour later with the biggest smile on my face. She was one of many girls who made it known they wanted a piece, so who was I to deny them? He thought it was hilarious, too that when we arranged to go out, I was always the first one at the meeting point and the last one to leave at the end of the night.

I was with Hackett once when after pre-season training we needed rehydrating. They all got Lucozade, Ribena and water. Mine was a Guinness. It never affected me. I was always at the front of the running. He liked the fact that I didn't come through the conventional ranks and saw me as a rough-cut diamond. I prided myself on getting my crosses in and always being effective. Despite my lifestyle, when I played I hated letting the side down. He loved that.

I went to Warren's wedding in Theydon Bois, north London, later in my career, turning up in a taxi around 5pm. There was no point in sending the driver away so I paid him to stay until I was ready to leave at 2am. Everyone thought I'd be heading home, but guess who ended up at the Emporium in the West End?

The Charisma nightclub in Doncaster was our favourite. My party piece was, as people were leaving, I would stand in the half-light near a post by the exit, pull out my dick for fun just to see the girls' reaction.

One boy noticed as he walked past with his girlfriend and was so amused he pulled her back to make sure she got a butcher's.

Ryan reckons all my girls then were fit. He remembers one in particular, Tracy, a blonde fitness instructor. We played at Barnet and she came to meet me. Everyone was asking who she was with and a few faces dropped when they saw her greet me. She was heavy.

* * * * *

There was a real buzz at Doncaster. We were playing well and attracting a lot of interest. Lots of scouts were coming to see us and it was inevitable some would get a big move. That season, 1994–95, we were on fire. We won 1-0 at Hereford. I set up a great goal for Bomber Jones. It was a heavy move. Then we beat Northampton 1-0 at home and Colchester 3-0 away. We were top of the league and having a laugh.

Paul Speller came to that Colchester game. Bomber got one and O'Neill Donaldson scored twice. Then it was Fulham at home. Their defender, Gary Brazil, tackled me and we both went down. Our legs were tangled up and, as I was getting up, I accidentally kicked him in the face, just a brush. Geezer rolled around like I'd shot him. The ref gave me a straight red card. Proper mad, I tried to get at him in the players' lounge, but got dragged away before I got myself into more trouble. I'm not known for being a dirty player and it hurt to be sent off for an offence I didn't commit. The FA must have believed me because I only got a one-match ban, the most lenient punishment. We did well to hold Fulham to a 0-0 draw with ten men. Had I stayed on, I'm sure we would have won.

At Torquay I scored with a wicked volley. Bad boy volley. Speller came with his missus, Clare. It was her birthday. Great treat for her, eh? My goal was her present. No woman could have been treated better. Then we went to Exeter. That place is long – it took seven hours by coach. At least we had the luxury of travelling the day before. Some teams, who can't afford it, leave in the early hours the morning of the game. Imagine how tired the players must be. No wonder Exeter's home record is good against financially struggling teams. We were flying them times and thrashed them 5-1.

A 3-0 win against Hartlepool followed before we drew 1-1 at Carlisle, who were a good side at the time. Yours truly scored ours. Mick Norbury bolted down the left, slipped it in, I came in and blasted it into the bottom left-hand corner. They equalised in the second half. It was a massive game with a crowd of nearly 8,000.

A 0-0 draw at Northampton was next. We were always in the top six, losing only twice in the first eighteen league matches. Then we lost 2-1 at home to Colchester and things started to go wobbly. I'd missed the Northampton game with a knee injury and came on as a sub against Colchester in horrible conditions. It was windy and they played a long-ball game.

We drew with Scunthorpe 1-1 at home and then it was away to Walsall, the league leaders – very eventful. Banter with fans is part and parcel of the game, everyone knows that it seems, except referees. Some take themselves and the game far too seriously. Just before half-time Brabs had got fed up of their fans taunting him about his size. He is average height but very stockily built, weighing around fourteen stone. Brabs fouled someone, pretty innocuous, but the crowd over-reacted and started chanting, 'You fat bastard! You fat bastard!' In a shirt he looks like a porker, but don't be fooled.

Never a retiring flower, Brabs lifted up his shirt to show a tight stomach. He used to be a bouncer and probably didn't want to go back to that way of life, so was always in shape. Six-pack? More like eight-pack! The crowd laughed, but just for that the muppet referee sent him off. We were furious. Walsall won 1-0 in a bad-tempered match and we felt that had Brabs not been sent off, things might have been different because we played well. To make matters worse, they came knocking on our door taunting us. Brabs flew out there swinging. I jumped up, but never got a chance to whack anyone because there were too many bodies. Their keeper Jimmy Walker said, 'You guys are a bunch of thugs.' But whose fault was it?

We lost five of the next six games and drew the other one. Our promotion hopes were slipping fast. 1-0 wins against Torquay and Exeter followed to halt the slide, but by then my attentions were directed elsewhere. Little did I know that less than two years after leaving the humiliation and misery of jail, my life was going to turn into a schoolboy's fairytale.

Chapter 8

PREMIER QUALITY

We were third in the league at Doncaster for a couple of months from October 1994. My form was excellent. Nuff clubs had been to watch me. Sheffield United and a few other clubs had shown interest, including Leicester, whose manager, Mark McGhee, needed a right-winger. Silky rang me in London and gave me the best news I'd ever heard: I was going to Leicester City in the Premiership. 'They want to sign you,' he said. 'The speculation is over.'

Of all the clubs interested, Leicester were the most exciting because they were actually in the Prem, albeit struggling. Next day I went up. I had a medical and trained with the boys. Then I went back to London to collect my things and returned to sign at Filbert Street for £125,000 with the fee rising to £250,000 depending on number of appearances. The feeling of elation was indescribable. In two eventful short years I'd gone from prison to the Premiership.

I had a mixture of emotions in joining Leicester, but Sammy Chung and George Smith made me believe I could do it – I'll always be grateful to them for that. That first weekend I went to a party at the Brixton Academy and met Lesley Grinter, who I'd grown up with, and saw she was still looking alright. It's easy to be attracted to Lesley: she's blonde, pretty with a nice figure and ready smile. I was with Kerrie that night, but sneaked off to get Lesley's number.

I was Mark McGhee's first signing: don't know how the move came along, Silky must have sold me to them. Played wicked in the reserves the next week. Them times 5,000 used to watch Leicester reserves. That was more than we were getting at Doncaster's first-team games. My head was more than spinning. Talk about excitement! I watched the Foxes beat Enfield 2-0 in the FA Cup. They hired me a car, I collected some things from Doncaster and they put me up in a hotel.

The first one I'd stayed at in Sunderland was plush but this one was five-star – proper: the Holiday Inn Country Club, just off junction 21 on the M1. I've stayed there a couple of times since and it's always a pleasure. The sense of déjà vu is amazing.

It was hard to take in at first. Some of the players I'd been seeing for years on TV were now my team-mates: Steve Walsh, Simon Grayson, Iwan Roberts,

Julian Joachim. Garry Parker and Mark Robins signed just after me. Robins is best known for saving Sir Alex Ferguson's job when struggling to establish himself as gaffer at Man United by scoring the only goal in the FA Cup Third Round against Nottingham Forest. Fergie would have been sacked if they'd lost, but United went on to win the cup that year, 1990, and gave him a reprieve.

The following week I played at Crystal Palace. It was 14 January 1994, the day I realised so many schoolboys' dreams of playing in the world's top league. Strangely though, I wasn't nervous beforehand. It was just another match as far as I was concerned, even though the crowd was much bigger than Doncaster's average of 3,000. We lost 2-0, but I did alright. The biggest difference from Third Division football was the quality of the passing: fewer balls given away. It was much faster, too and everyone's first touch was at a higher level.

Next week we were at Manchester City. It was chucking down. I set up the winner for Robins and we won 1-0. I told the Leicester City fanzine *Blue Army News*: 'I've been reasonably satisfied but I know I can still do a lot better. I have plenty to learn and this is only the start. Despite the conditions, which were the worst I've ever played in, I really enjoyed the match. My only disappointment was that I didn't score a few minutes earlier. I thought my header was on its way into the net and couldn't believe it that Andy Dibble saved it.' Mark McGhee was full of praise, too. He said, 'I thought Jamie had an excellent match. He worked hard all the way through and really got stuck into his defensive duties, as well as getting forward and causing them problems. It was the sort of performance I knew he was capable of producing, but I thought we were unlikely to see it for another six months while he was settling down and adjusting to this level of football.' Glowing praise, but as if to stop me from getting too full of myself, I was dropped.

* * * * *

McGhee put me on the subs bench for the next match against West Ham, which we lost 2-1 at home. Then it was Arsenal away, where we drew 1-1. It was great playing at Highbury, which has so much history and all that, but nothing really sticks out in my mind about the place, players and game. People say I must have been very excited and nervous, but I didn't feel any of those things. Playing at places like Old Trafford, Goodison Park and Stamford Bridge was just like any other ground, only bigger with more fans. Only Anfield really got me excited and that's because as a kid I supported Liverpool. I suppose the anti-climax stemmed from the fact that we were going to be relegated anyway and there was a gloom about the place that only winning and avoiding the drop could lift.

I ended up playing seventeen times for Leicester that season, eight as sub and scored one league goal. My celebrity in Battersea had soared, even though my attitude remained the same. I was still a regular in the Beaufoy Arms, though it was getting more expensive because everyone expected me to buy the drinks. Football was all they wanted to talk about, which was irritating 'cos I liked to get away from it, and every armchair expert in the area approached me with their theories on every aspect of the game when all I wanted was to get away from the sport. It was suffocating. The media attention was cool still. I took that in my stride and was careful with what I said to the Press because they like to twist things; had to have my wits about me. All Premiership players are wary of the Press – they can do so much damage if they catch you out. An unguarded comment at the wrong time can land you in a lot of trouble, not just with the manager but the club, too. Just ask Lee Sharpe, who got a major bollocking from his manager, Alex Ferguson, in December 1990, just for going on record saying it was nice scoring a hat-trick against bitter rivals Arsenal in Man United's 6-2 win. That was a few years ago, but it still sticks out in the players' minds for its unfairness. No wonder Sharpey eventually left.

Leicester finished twenty-first and, with Palace, Norwich and Ipswich, in May 1995 we were relegated. It was disappointing going down, but I was sure we could make it back to the Premiership, ideally with a better manager than McGhee, who may have signed me, but did not have the full respect of the players or fans.

Going to Sunderland with Leicester for the first game of the 1995–96 season was interesting for the memories. Their fans gave me a warm reception when I went on as sub, even though I'd only played there five times. It was all the more enjoyable because we won 2-1. I started the next game, at home to Stoke City. Played well, but we lost 3-2. McGhee partly blamed me and I got dropped, even though he tried to play me at wingback, which I wasn't happy with. I went to see him and he reassured me that I was definitely in his plans. The next week I weren't even on the bench.

Little did I know this would be his last match of playing mind games with me because he walked out on the club to manage Wolves, our arch-rivals. There was a lot of bitterness about that, but some of us were not that bothered because we didn't really rate him, unlike his successor Martin O'Neill.

They were hard times for me because I was commuting from London every day and my personal life was in turmoil. I got two girls – Tasha and Lesley – pregnant at the same time. There had been a lot of speculation that McGhee would walk out. I was 'ill' for ten days when the news broke. At the time I couldn't handle the football with the personal stress. The best thing about playing for McGhee was when he joined Wolves at the end of 1995. He had a history of doing that, having left Reading for Leicester the previous year. He's still bouncing around from club to club now with varying success.

I weren't living right, travelling back to London every day. I know I should have moved to Leicester but the pull to be with my bredrens was too strong. I went in to see O'Neill and he said, 'Your reputation goes before you, but as far as I'm concerned, the slate is clean. You don't know us and we don't know you.' They saw me in training, how I got stuck in and worked my bollocks off. O'Neill always likes commitment and I think I impressed him very quickly. As long as I tried he loved me.

When I got to Leicester I was still seeing Kerrie. I rang Lesley in the week. She was working in the King's Road, Chelsea. Within a month of starting to see Lesley, she got pregnant. There was a girl working for Ambrose Mendy that I liked, too: Siobhan. Once, I arranged to see both of them on the same day at Leicester; I thought I had planned it like a military operation. Lesley was in my hotel room and Siobhan rang to say she was just leaving London. But Lesley took the call and messed it up. I missed out – Siobhan was alright.

*****

Looking back, I fucked up at Leicester because I didn't fully appreciate the chance. I went out too much and was still immature. I behaved like a young kid of eighteen, nineteen, who'd just got a contract. I used to take ten-day sickies just to go partying.

It will surprise many to hear how much I've changed since. I met my partner Rowena in a nightclub in Battersea. Nuff man was after her. She had attitude, but my attitude at the time was that chicks were ten a penny. I've calmed down since meeting her, even though she doesn't think so. Our daughter, Tiagh, was born on 23 April 2002 and she's helped me to change a lot. I used to be twenty times worse, running down every girl I fancied, but not anymore. Rowena, a trainee beautician, has captured my heart.

At least my son Nathan, who was born exactly four months after my daughter Tamara in 1996, is constant in my life. Me and him have a bond still. I thank Tash for bringing him up the right way and not trying to use him as a pawn because things didn't work out between us. She's been as good as gold. He's a hyperactive kid, just like I was at that age, and whenever I ring to ask to have him, she says, 'Fine, I could do with the break!' They live in Wandsworth Common and I love taking him out, to parties, football. He's a mini-me and because he loves to fight, he might be a boxer, if not a footballer. Whenever I take him to parties, he's always the one fighting. I don't want him to be a bully, but then again he must stand up for himself. He's skinny, but wiry and, just like me, is never afraid to defend himself.

We had a little problem recently. These older boys were picking on him. I went round and spoke to the parents politely. But the trouble continued. So I went round there and this time I got a little dark on them. I told all the dads that if their boys continued putting their hands on mine then I would have to put my hands on them. The next time it happened the dads wouldn't open their doors and they called the police. We haven't had any trouble from them since.

Around the time Lesley got pregnant I had a clash with a local bad boy, Trevor Barkworth. His mum, Elsie, had told Lesley that I was staying with Tasha. That's how she turned up at Tasha's when I was out. Lesley went round to Tasha's before she got pregnant. Lesley was shouting the odds that they were going to fight. Tasha's sister sorted it out. Elsie Barkworth was always a nosy busybody. It had absolutely nothing to do with her. She was always getting in other people's business. We were in a club called Wessex House and I told Trevor to have a word with his mum because she was out of order. His sister Tracy admitted to me: 'Mum was wrong.'

Because Trevor got drunk, he turned rude boy and tried to start something inside. The bouncers threw him out. Tracy pleaded with me to leave it. An hour and a half later I came out. My cousin Mark went out first. He came back and told me Trevor was waiting for me outside and to just walk past him, ignore him. 'Yeah, I'll do the bigger man thing,' I said. I walked past Trevor, who was shouting all this racist abuse. But it was too much. I gave him one raas right. He crumpled and started bawling like a bitch. Mark said, 'He deserved that; he took your kindness for weakness.' His brother-in-law, Darren Bright, was a bad boy, but Trevor wasn't. Thought he could have it with me 'cos of Darren. It doesn't go like that.

* * * * *

In my early Leicester days I used to room with a talented kid who had just burst into the first team. A big, strong striker, he had exceptional touch, a terrific shot and seemed destined for a bright future. Sure enough, he went on to establish himself in the side, became an England international and got an £11 million transfer to Liverpool. Emile Heskey is at Birmingham now and although we don't get a chance to see each other often, we speak regularly. He deserved all his England caps and should get more, despite what people say of him.

Martin O'Neill's previous club was Norwich, but he left there on principle. He felt they got him there under false pretences because they weren't prepared to spend. O'Neill came with his coaching team: Steve Walford, Paul Franklin and John Robertson. His coaching staff is quality, too. Walford is a naturally funny man – he'd do crazy things for a laugh. Once he'd be taking us at five-a-side in the pouring rain.

After a good while we realised that he hadn't whistled. He'd long gone to the changing room. 'This one's a mad man,' I thought. Anyone late for training would get fined a fiver or tenner, depending on how late they were. He'd be standing there, collecting it, saying: 'Nice – that'll pay for my fags... I'll get a bottle of whisky with that.' He had a good-looking daughter and we joked that we would take her out. Walford said to me: 'Fuckin' hell, you'll give me a heart attack! I don't mind Emile Heskey going out with her, he's got money, but you'll ruin her.'

O'Neill, a very shrewd, clever Irishman, saw it through in the tough, early days at Leicester. He's a straight-up person, no airs or graces. You just can't go wrong if you listen and respect him. To show you what a quality guy he is, he left managing Celtic to attend to his sick wife, and the rest of his coaching team left, too. That's class. He's a people's person, always looked after his teams, anything he had to say would stay in the club. We were a bunch of lunatics, almost as crazy as the Doncaster lads. All of us went out together and as long as we weren't too out of order and did the business on the pitch, O'Neill didn't interfere. This is someone who learnt the business during his playing days, mostly at Nottingham Forest under Brian Clough, who had played in the World Cup finals for Northern Ireland and must have known every trick in the book. This was going to be a battle of wits and I was sure I could get the better of him...

Chapter 9

REVENGE ON THE BACKSTABBER

In my first game for Martin O'Neill I played wingback at home to Portsmouth, the team winning 4-2. For the next game he didn't have to gee us up: it was Wolves. We were buzzing from the adrenaline. Everyone wanted to stick it to Martin McGhee, our recently departed former manager, who had just walked out on us to a higher bidder, no sense of loyalty. We felt Martin was a backstabber, even though he kept trying to justify what he did. He showed Leicester no respect and we were prepared to die that day to prove our point. If I bumped into him now I would be polite because he brought me into the Premiership. I'm not bitter; it was just the sneaky way he went about it. We won 1-0.

Our form was patchy under O'Neill in the early days of that 1995–96 season. To be fair, he was trying to get to know the players before he brought his own in. Like all good managers, he was friendly enough, but kept his distance a bit so as not to lose respect. Imagine our surprise then when we went to Oldham and he ordered us to meet him in the bar the night before the game. Tension was high. Everybody was sitting around quietly, waiting for him to come in, expecting to be read the riot act about discipline, tactics, honouring the name of the club, whatever. The mood was gloomy.

'Now, who wants a drink?' asked O'Neill happily. I was the first to put up my hand: 'Pint of Guinness, please.' That really broke the ice. Mindful of impressing the new boss, everyone started to leave early for bed. As I stood up, O'Neill said: 'You're staying here with me.' He wanted to know all about my past, so from then we were rapping alright. O'Neill is a very intelligent man with a huge interest in law; he even attended the Peter Sutcliffe trial to try and work out the psycho's logic. We lost to Oldham 3-1, but the session the night before wasn't the cause. After that icebreaker we went out there, wanting to do well for O'Neill. Oldham was just the better team on the day.

Martin O'Neill instilled in us that a game is never lost until that final whistle. He kept us hungry. If anyone got complacent, he would go mad. But he was very fair. Never held grudges, and when he said something to you that was the end of it. Whenever I see him now, he hugs me up.

We were third when he took over that January, but for the first ten games, mainly draws, we just could not win for love nor money. Neil Lennon and Muzzy Izzet joined soon after and when they settled in, they turned out to be special guys. Mark McGhee liked the diamond formation, but O'Neill preferred three at the back with two wingbacks, three in midfield and two up front. In the early days he kept getting hate mail. Everyone was calling for his head, but he stayed calm and stuck to what he was doing. But we slipped down to mid-table. O'Neill was getting even more abuse in the post. Some feared that we would be relegated. Many wrote he was out of his depth and should leave with dignity immediately. He kept all the letters and held on, defying the pressure. Then we started to gel.

After a faltering start, O'Neill and his brilliant back-up team got us winning at last. In May 1996 we even reached the play-offs against all expectations. When we got into the play-offs I was on another ten-day sickie. With two new-born kids in south London my mind was totally elsewhere. Reaching the play-offs excited me and I decided that I fancied playing again. But when the gaffer saw me approaching with another lame excuse he didn't even bother to hear me out: 'Jamie, fuck off.' He knew I was trying to get in the play-offs. I'd pissed him off. I collected my things as it was end of season and wasn't too worried as I had a year left on my contract. We faced Palace and won 2-1. Steve Claridge scored the winner. I was watching on TV and cheering, not only because we'd won but because the promotion meant I had twenty grand coming.

* * * * *

Lesley getting pregnant so quickly surprised me. She was mad, used to try to attack me. When I came to London I wanted to see my mates, but she would say, 'No, you're not going nowhere.' One day I got in my car to go out with the lads and she lay on the bonnet to stop me. We were staying at her sister's house in Guildford at the time so I coaxed her back in the house to talk it over. I came on like James Bond and jumped out of the window, then drove off. I laughed all the way to the Beaufoy Arms and had just settled down to a session with my old friend Guinness when she turned up. She'd jumped on the train. Another time she tried to smash the windscreen of my car with her handbag to stop me going out: crazy woman.

Once Paul Speller and my boys came to the hotel I was staying in. Lesley was going on with her mad self and her pet hamster in a cage. When she left the room, I had a bottle of wine and, out of frustration, I poured it over the hamster and kicked the cage. It died. When she came back, she was running up her mouth that I'd killed her hamster. Speller pretended it was still alive, took it to his car and said he would look after it in

London. She believed him, not knowing that Speller threw it out on the motorway.

Even her dad said he was surprised I was staying with her. Once she dashed all my clothes from the boot of the car. She got loud man! I centrally locked myself in, but she managed to open the boot and pull out the clothes. Another time, I went to Richmond with Speller and the boys. I went back to Battersea to get my car, but she had stolen the keys from her parents' house in Surrey Lane, where my car was. She was running all over the Surrey Lane Estate with the keys, with her mum and dad chasing after her. It all ended at the police station and they gave me the keys the next day. I had to get someone to move my BMW away so that it didn't get towed.

The other girl I got pregnant at that time was Tasha. Over the years she made my heart strings tug. First, Lesley got pregnant, then Tasha four months later. They lived close to each other. What a nightmare! One day Lesley was in the Dunston Estate and I was trying to avoid her. Tasha, my ex-girlfriend, beckoned me in to hide in her place, and I never left after that. She knew Lesley was pregnant. One day I got back from training and saw a pregnancy test kit. 'Who's is this?' I asked. She replied, 'Oh, it's my sister's.' That didn't ring true. Tasha put a piece of paper in my pocket. Rah! Pregnancy test positive. I'd gone twenty-six years childless, then bang! It was like London buses, two at once.

I went round to see Lesley, who was heavily pregnant, to tell her. Someone had told her I was living in the next street, Gideon Road. She took the news badly and started going round there, causing trouble. Tasha told me to sort it out. By now Kerrie was completely out of the picture and I was also seeing Donna at the time. She was a proper babe, a Halle Berry lookalike. Donna had a man at the time and left him for me. In the end I finished it because of Tasha. Donna already had a little boy and I knew she wanted a long-term relationship, but with two kids on the way in London and Donna 200 miles away, it would have been too much juggling.

Lesley gave birth to Tamara on 2 February 1996 at the Chelsea and Westminster Hospital. When I went to see them it was a weird atmosphere, but the family knew the score. I've not had the best relationship with Tamara, mainly because I've had her mother to deal with. After a while Lesley had another kid with someone else. She would let me see Tamara for a couple of months, then stop access. Lesley would say I could see her on the Sunday, then I'd go round there with my mum and Tamara wouldn't be there, but Lesley couldn't give a reasonable explanation.

The last time I went to see Tamara was in 2001. I parked up and could see Lesley in her kitchen. She knew I was coming and must have seen me. When I knocked on her front door, there was no answer: she was obviously pretending she was out. She must have looked through the spy-hole and decided not to let me in. I'd had enough of her childish games.

Lesley was also jealous of my relationship with Nathan. I used to take him round there to see his sister, but Lesley made things difficult. Her man was giving me dirty looks behind her back. I felt like knocking him out, but just left it. She likes men she can rule over. Amazingly, she got pregnant by me again, but I told her directly that I was not going through that again. She wisely got rid of it.

It was a strange time when the two women had their babies because I was with Tasha and if we had an argument, then I would just go to Lesley's round the corner and chill. That's when I knocked her up again. The anger is still there, despite the years. Lesley got the Child Support Agency after me. She would have got more money if she hadn't gone down that route. After I stopped seeing Tamara, I used to buy her cards and presents, and have kept them all so when she gets big enough to come and find me, she will know that I never stopped loving her and wanting to be a part of her life.

* * * * *

The distractions affected my football and, looking back, I might have been an even better player had I not partied so much. During all that madness I was seeing someone else, on and off as well. To save her blushes, let's call her Miss X. It ended in 2000. We had been seeing each other on a casual basis for nine years, but I knew it could never be permanent because she was too fiery: she was a girl version of me. When it came to sex, she was a freak. The sex was off-the-wall. She loved role-playing in the most bizarre way. One of her favourites was that I had to sneak into her house with a knife, wearing all black and a mask, and pretend to attack her like a rapist. She also liked pretending to walk an imaginary dog in the park. Hiding behind the bushes, I would have to jump out, chase her and we'd do it right there on Wandsworth Common. Also, she liked me to drive really, really fast to Boxhill whilst she gave me oral sex. When we arrived, she would spread herself across the bonnet and I'd give it to her right there. Dressing up as a nurse was another theme. I would walk into the 'surgery' and she would say, 'Good morning, Mr Lawrence, how are you today?' I would reply, 'Well, Nurse Kitty, I've got an ache in my groin, can you help?' Her name would change every time. Other times she would play the prostitute and I had to be the punter. It was wild and sordid, and very exciting. With all that al fresco sex, I'm just glad that the police never nicked me!

Miss X had a good heart. She was always charming to my Mum and the rest of the family around and nothing was too much trouble for her. She worked in an estate agent's, a very prim and proper job, and acted as if butter wouldn't melt in her mouth. Behind closed doors, she was a tiger. Well, not always behind closed doors...

Miss X came up for Christmas and, as I couldn't cook, I phoned and got loads of Yardie food: Jerk chicken, ricen'peas, plantain, hard dough bread, the whole nine yards. I bought some candles and did the whole romantic rude boy bit. We went to Paris for a romantic weekend and did the tourist thing, visiting the Eiffel Tower and Euro Disney. I found a restaurant and had flowers and champagne waiting at our table. The highlight of that trip was doing it on our hotel balcony in broad daylight as we looked at the Eiffel Tower. She couldn't get enough of me.

Miss X was very jealous. Handling her volatile nature was the only drawback. We had a big argument after she tried to attack me just because I'd said hello to my agent's girlfriend. Miss X dashed a drink in my agent's girlfriend's face because she was jealous. Then she tried to fight me. It was at the Emporium in the West End, just behind Hamley's toy shop. We went outside to talk it out and she flew at me again. Not wanting to hit her, I pushed her onto the black bin bags on the kerb. She calmed down a little and we got into a taxi. Miss X told the driver I had attacked her, but he looked at me and said, 'If he wanted to beat you up, it would be all over your face now, love.' When we got to Ray Grant's flat in Battersea, she started again, so I poured water all over her. She left, and that was the end of the relationship.

I missed her, but we were both stubborn and the relationship had run its course: the grief outweighed the wild sex.

* * * * *

Being a reasonably well-known footballer has its perks with the girls. The attention is enjoyable but sometimes, as a team man, you have to Take One For The Team. That's when a mate pulls and she's got a mate, and out of obligation you have to Take One For The Team. Jamaicans have a term for fat, ugly girls: 'mampies'. Luckily, I didn't have to deal with them too often. They had only one visit, too, unlike some team-mates, who couldn't always shake off their new, fat squeeze. My girls had to have something going on. If the face wasn't quite right, the figure had to be correct.

It may come as a big shock to some readers, but footballers get more than the average opportunity for sexual encounters. It's a perk of the job. Like the time I went to Tenerife with Paul Speller and a Leicester player. We met a group of girls at the hotel's swimming pool and I started a fling with Adèle from Manchester. The highlight of that being us getting it on in the pool. Speller and I went out separately and he'd lost his room key. He climbed up to the balcony and saw me on top of a girl, and remembers her boots in the air. Speller went away for a couple of hours and when he returned, he could not believe I was still banging her. So he had a joint on the balcony and waited for us to finish. That was a wicked holiday.

Speller was with me the time I picked up two girls when I was parked on a red route in Leicester in a flash BMW. They got in, and Speller was talking politely to the one I didn't fancy. But she was really lairy. They quickly started arguing and he kicked her out. I'd just joined Leicester and was staying in a hotel then, and started banging my girl with Speller fast asleep in an adjoining room. In the morning I tried to wake him to move to digs, but he wouldn't budge, so I left. He woke up later and came into my room. She was fast asleep naked and I had emptied the room and moved into digs, leaving her with a £10 note to get a taxi home. I couldn't stand facing her in the morning and going through that charade about wanting to see her again.

Speller lives in Coulsdon now and is settled with his wife Clare and his two beautiful girls. I'm godfather to one, and Ray's godfather to the other. But he enjoyed some wild nights in his younger days. Speller, Mark Hills and one of my cousins came to Winston's in Leeds. They couldn't understand how the only women in there were real stunners in their underwear. I was used to the scene and played pool that night. My mates couldn't believe it when these gorgeous girls tapped them on the shoulder and said, 'Your mate's just paid for me to be with you.' They got the girls back to their hotel. I paid them to expose themselves and one sucked me off. By now it was breakfast time and even though my mates were exhausted, I insisted on treating them to a full English served with Budweiser. It was my birthday and I wanted to make the most of the occasion. One girl declared in front of embarrassed guests that sex with me was the best she'd ever had. It was a great birthday!

Speller is more than a friend: he's like an extra brother. For example, one time at a police station waiting to go to jail, he took my girlfriend Aloisa there. The cops were cool and even used to go out and get me takeaways. Even in custody they were obliging enough to ignore me for an hour whilst I entertained Aloisa.

Speller's seen so many crazy things, like when a bad boy pulled a gun on me. I beat up a guy called Ben Milton. I was getting some Ralph Lauren clothes and selling them on. This guy was not coming up with the money he owed and always coming up with excuses. I got fed up with him taking the piss and went round Dunston Estate and beat him up outside his cousin's house.

Another time some brother called Jamie Porter, who used to hang around Ben Milton, called me up and said he wanted a peaceful word. I went round there and a stranger pulled out a shotgun on me. I ran off, but he couldn't have been that tough because he was so nervous he dropped it. Ten minutes later the gunman, who recognised me from our schooldays, rang me and said it was all a misunderstanding. I reckon Jamie Porter and Ben Milton were giving him drugs to keep him mellow. I went to meet him in a Battersea pub an hour later. He was really apologetic. He got his comeuppance later because he is now crippled after being shot. In a roundabout way he got touched, and it was someone I knew.

The second time I had a gun pulled on me was in the Coliseum nightclub in Vauxhall in August 2000. My bredren, a proper wide boy, used to bad up the bouncers proper. He would stand at the entrance and decide who was coming in and who wasn't. They hated and feared him in equal measure, and by association, me, too. One night I went there with my girlfriend and the bouncers recognised me. 'You're not coming in,' one said. 'Why not?' I replied. I stood my ground and got in. Embarrassed, the bouncer decided to take things further and appeared on the dance floor brandishing a silver gun at me. People who knew both of us jumped in to quell the situation as others fled, screaming. He really had issues with me. Two-twos, we left. Still fuming, I went back the same night looking for revenge. He wasn't there and one of his mates said to leave it. Nothing came of it, but I continued going to the club, hoping to see him. The bouncers were fed up of getting bad up by my mate, who is still my friend to this day.

* * * *

It was an exciting time. Being with a big club like Leicester gave me a sense of achievement and helped fill the emptiness and despair of those bad-boy years. Being a good father to two new-borns was challenging but it gave me a sense of perspective. Earning decent dough and getting recognised for things not connected with badness boosted my ego. Leicester had got back in the Premiership. Life was so good I felt blessed. There was only one nagging doubt in my mind: Would I get the chance to establish myself in O'Neill's improving team at the highest level?

Chapter 10

AGAINST ALL EXPECTATIONS

Martin O'Neill brought in American keeper Kasey Keller that summer of 1996. He was better than the keepers we already had, but I found him a bit stuck up. He never mixed with the rest. Once, at the Christmas do, he only drank water for two hours, and then left: very unsociable. Steve Walsh was more than a nutter. He led by example, was totally fearless. There was a game against Wimbledon when Walsh and Mick Harford, another hard man, were at it hammer and tongs throughout the game. As we were coming off the pitch Walsh thought it was going to kick off in the tunnel. He called me over and said, 'Jamie, watch my back.' I replied, 'No problem.' Nothing happened, though, because Harford had already gone. From that incident I knew I had his respect. It really felt good because Walsh was a Leicester legend.

Steve Claridge was a quality player at Leicester. His favourite story about me is the time he had one of the directors' cars, an Alpha Omega. I was drunk, but persuaded him to let me drive it down the M1. I wanted to test the turbo-boost and was reaching about 150mph from Leicester to Luton. He still tells that story to this day. The most frightening experience of his life, he says. How we didn't get nicked is a mystery.

Years later, when I was at Brentford, Claridge joined and he was still talking about it. He is an entertaining guy, but odd. Claridge never cleaned his boots, his socks were always rolled down, and he hated shin pads. He loved betting on anything. His auto-biography admits it in graphic detail. I never got into that culture. My only bet was a £20 football accumulator every weekend – won me a grand in April 2005. I don't mind losing a score, but I was never a card player like some. I played for only a fiver a hand and £20 was my limit, but I've seen players lose on shoot pontoon for massive stakes. On a trip I've seen people losing grands. I could never play for big dough as I'd feel too guilty taking that much money off a mate; that's low. Many did it out of boredom, for a bit of excitement, but not me.

The best left-back I faced them times was Tony Dorigo at Leeds. He had everything – pace, good feet and courage. Julian Dicks at West Ham was very competitive, too. I took him on twice, beat him and, on the third time, he knew what was coming. He whacked me. I started laughing. 'What you laughing at, you fucking idiot?' he asked. But he was alright, played with the right spirit.

Stuart Pearce was also a good player. I admired his never-say-die attitude and expect him to do well now he's a manager. David Ginola was brilliant the times I played against him. So, too, was Dennis Bergkamp. He scored the best hat trick ever when we drew 4-4 with Arsenal. I was on the bench and still remember all three of his goals perfectly. One hit the stanchion from the edge of the box, another came after he flicked it over a geezer's head, and the geezer's still running for it now. The third was another blinder. Ian Wright kicked me hard once when we played Arsenal. Talk about excitable – he's a livewire.

I didn't feel out of place playing against big names because from childhood self-belief was instilled in me by Pete Rhodes, the coach from my youth. He used to watch me on TV, playing in right midfield. Although Martin O'Neill is considered one of the game's most astute football brains, Pete reckoned I was out of position and should have been playing in central midfield. He used to say, 'You're like Bobby Moore, James, looking to pass the ball before you've even received it. You've got great vision but it's wasted playing there.'

There were some great times at Leicester. One Christmas we had a fancy dress party and after a couple of drinks someone dared me to get my cock out in a group photo for the local paper. Not until the photo had been distributed to all the wives and girlfriends a week later did they realise what I'd done. We were waiting for it to come out in the local paper, but someone must have spotted it and it never appeared. But the pic managed to find its way into a fanzine...

* * * * *

In my first full season at Leicester, 1996–97 we had a great Coca-Cola Cup run. We faced little Scarborough over two legs in the First Round. In the home leg I scored one of those goals that are shown on a BBC's *Question of Sport*'s round: 'What Happened Next?' Someone drove the ball across very low. It was begging to be booted in, but I stooped down and headed it in as a defender's boot hit me full on. I'd scored, but been knocked unconscious. As I was being stretchered off, Muzzy Izzet goes, 'Are you alright, Jamie?' Typically, my only thought was winning: 'Did I score?' He was amazed. Heskey said, 'Nobody but Jamie could have scored like that.' O'Neill was ecstatic that someone could be so brave. Or was it foolish?

With commitment like that Martin O'Neill was convinced I finally had the right attitude: I was a regular from there. But I weren't making much money. Commuting from London was getting exhausting; seeing two babies by different mothers was draining. Once I got on a train from London to Milton Keynes, where I was supposed to meet some team-mates. But I was late and they'd already left. I got a cab from Milton Keynes to the training camp. Cost a fortune. When I saw Walford, I asked him how much my fine was. 'No, this time you made the effort,' he said. 'No fine.'

Towards the end of my Leicester days in early 1997 I was also seeing Donna. She worked with nursery kids, had a little girl of her own and wanted to settle down seriously. But I just couldn't make the commitment.

With so many distractions, it's no wonder Martin O'Neill did not pick me regularly in the early days. He probably wanted to keep me hungry, desperate to play and not complacent. For example, I had one of my finest games in a 4-2 win over Derby playing wingback. I did really well and expected to be a regular after that, but I was dropped to sub for the next game. Though disappointed, I wasn't devastated because his first-choice team was doing well. Managers often have it in their heads what is their best team. Rightly or wrongly, they like to keep their favourites in, but if he'd given me a chance, there was no way I was going to rest on my laurels.

We faced the mighty Manchester United in the Coca-Cola Cup next. Paul Scholes and Roy Keane were playing, so they were taking it pretty seriously: proper players with some youngsters thrown in. Even if it was a weakened team, it didn't matter: we were desperate to win. I came on and gave away a penalty with my first challenge; went up for a header and fouled Keane. Thankfully, Scholes missed the kick. That's the only penalty I've ever given away. Against all expectations, we won 2-0. I zoomed down the M1 back to London in record time. Door-to-door, it only took me sixty-five minutes. How I didn't get pulled, I don't know. Everything was blessed that night, things were running nicely.

I played in all but one round of the Coca-Cola Cup and then Scott Taylor came back from injury. He was selected for the final at Wembley against Middlesbrough. That broke my heart. All my friends and family were there. Heskey scored a last-minute equaliser to force a replay. Before the replay I played against Arsenal at Highbury and had a wicked match, even though we lost 2-0. It earned me a place on the bench in the replay at Hillsborough. Before the match, I was warming up with Muzzy Izzet and we started playfighting. I got him in a headlock and my long fingernails cut his face open. It really hurt him: 'Fuck that, Jamie. I wouldn't like to be your enemy.

We used to travel on trains to and from London together. After training Muzzy would ask for a coke. I'd return from the buffet with one and a Carlsberg four-pack (always polished it off before we arrived in

London). Muzzy would shake his head in disbelief. He said, 'I hate you Jamie! You've got the body of a twenty-one-year-old, drink like a fish, shag everything that moves, and you can still play a bit!'

Once Muzzy was pestered by a thug at the Holiday Inn after a Sheffield Wednesday game. Some geezer was really giving it to him and things were getting nasty. I put it to him: 'Let's go outside and I'll wipe the floor with you.' He skulked away. I'm always looking out for anyone I care for. No one's ever got the better of me in a one-on-one – I suppose it's a confidence thing.

Coming on in the last twenty minutes guaranteed me a place in cup history, even if we lost. Thankfully, Claridge scored in the last minute for our 1-0 win. Against the odds, not only had we stayed in the Prem by finishing a respectable tenth, we'd also got into Europe by winning the Coca-Cola Cup. All the pundits were wrong.

The last game of the season was at Blackburn. The night before, we were all on the piss and expected to get thrashed. It was a celebration weekend and a little thing like a Premiership match was never going to get in the way of our enjoyment. Damien Duff was coming through them times for Blackburn. There must have been eight or nine pints in me that day but because it was away, we'd had a fantastic season and there was no pressure, we just played for fun – and won 4-2. Great relief! Even our own fans expected us to go down that season.

We put our success down to Martin O'Neill. He doesn't really coach, but he knows how to put a team together. O'Neill later revealed he had kept all the hate mail and wrote back to all of them. Even now he should get the Freedom of the City. Had he stayed, Leicester might now be one of the Premiership's best, no doubt.

Heskey who's not a drinker, got drunk inside half an hour on champagne. He puked up on the bus and his dad had to come and get him. We got lean up: very, very drunk; went on an open-top bus the next day. I hired a stretch limo from Wandsworth Common. It was the first time I'd ever been in a limo, thought I was the bollocks. I went up there in style with some of my boys: Brendon Bartlett, Darren Hendricks and Donny. We were busting champagne in there – wicked time. They came onto the bus and were going on like they'd played in the final themselves. Some supporters were asking, 'Who the fuck are they?'

I had a party in the Beaufoy Arms. Loads of pictures, blue-and-white ribbons everywhere. It was a proper night – Guinness, champagne, everything… People tipped us to go down, but we proved them wrong on every count.

They were a great bunch of lads. Matt Elliott, big, tough centre-back is the nicest geezer you could ever meet. Colin Hill was a great pro. You never saw him drunk – he loved going to work. Muzzy Izzet is a typical Cockney from Mile End, east London. He loved a drink almost as much as me, what a player. Izzet should have got an England call-up. Pontus Kamark was a Swede, who loved black girls. He loved to roll with black people – another brilliant pro. Kamark marked Juninho out of both games in the Coca-Cola Cup final that April.

Neil Lennon is the maddest Irishman I know, talk about stereotype. He loved to drink till he was in a coma. On holiday in Magaluf I was looking out my window and saw someone in a sombrero so drunk he was bouncing off the walls. It was Lennon. During the day he was always drinking by the pool, but was never sober enough to come out that night. Neil Lewis was a good kid. So much ability it was frightening, but he never realised his potential. Martin O'Neill worked his bollocks off, trying to get the best out of him. Ian Marshall was one of the few I didn't see eye-to-eye with for personal reasons, nor Spencer Prior who was a bit of a prick. He never socialised.

I thought Scott Taylor was an annoying little bastard: always hyper, like an irritating mosquito. He had all this excess energy and always wanted to play-fight. What a pest! He never wanted to chill out, so one day I just gave him a haymaker right to the chest. Decked him! He never troubled me again. Kevin Poole and Mike Whitlow were two of the nicest players at Leicester. Mike was a model pro who'd do anything for you, like going out of his way to drop me at the train station. Little things like that go a long way.

Jimmy Willis was the club's hypochondriac. According to him, none of his injuries warranted less than a major operation. A Scouser, he didn't mind admitting he lived in a caravan. I don't think he liked living away from Liverpool.

Leicester gave me a taster for the big-time. O'Neill offered me a new one-year contract but he wanted me to live in Leicester, even though he admitted he couldn't guarantee me a first-team place. He was totally honest and said if I didn't want to sign, then a few clubs were interested in me and he was prepared to let me go for a modest fee of £50,000. I went home to think about it. The following Monday I told him I wanted first-team football and would go. True to his word, he let me go and that June Bradford City came in for me.

Ironically, three weeks after I left, Simon Grayson, who was keeping me out of the team, moved to Aston Villa. Every time I went back to Leicester, O'Neill said, 'You should have stayed.' I was gutted 'cos I missed the team spirit and the club, and had really enjoyed my time at Leicester, but there was no use regretting.

The move came from nowhere. I was actually on holiday in Jamaica with Tasha and Nathan when Silky rang. We were staying in Trelawny and I signed by fax. I was really impressed with Bradford's eagerness. They obviously rated me. Bradford doubled my wages to £2,000 a week.

Steve Walford was sorry to see me go. I'd built up a great rapport with the coach. He knew my past and how I had a reputation for partying. I got back in the team through pure honesty and hard work. Steve identified with me because he had grown up in a rough part of Islington and Holloway, north London, and could have gone off the rails too, but found his salvation in football.

Steve knew I was tough, but not how hardheaded I was until I scored that diving header which knocked me out. 'You still went out for a drink that night,' he still laughs. He enjoyed fining us, especially the Londoners, for being late. But because he lived in Potters Bar, Hertfordshire, which is not far out of north London, he was very understanding. Steve was a real player's coach; he didn't mind my Guinness consumption and antics as long as I delivered on the pitch. He appreciated how well I did and, just like a lot of coaches and managers, liked the fact that I didn't moan when I was not in the team. Leaving Leicester was hard, but Jamie Lawrence had new horizons to conquer...

Chapter 11

BANTAMS WELCOME

Stepping off the plane from a holiday in Jamaica, refreshed and rested, my life was changing for the better after all the turmoil from my bad boy days. Within a couple of days I was in Bradford. Initially, it wasn't appealing. Bradford is 200 miles north of London and I was hoping to get a move back south from Leicester. Having already got to know every service station and junction exit along the M1, I was now going nearly a hundred miles further north. All I knew about the city was that it was in Yorkshire, near the Moors, and far away from London.

Being the only club in Bradford, fans are even more passionate than in bigger places, reflected by the fact that Bantam supporters were one of the first clubs to create their own fanzine, *City Gent*, in 1984. Bradford's prospects were not too hot when I joined.

They had just avoided relegation to Division Two and, even with the usual summer signings, their future didn't look that great. I'd been in two minds about whether or not to leave Leicester 'cos even though I wasn't a regular, I felt there was a chance with a great manager like Martin O'Neill and his back-up staff. The team was going to flourish and I wanted to be part of that.

Bradford manager Chris Kamara came to see me play for Leicester reserves and he liked what he saw. Although he was not convinced because I was drifting in and out of the games, he saw enough in me to make an offer if the terms were right. When Silky told him £50,000 he said, 'You're joking! I thought you were going to say £250,000.' At the time players with a lot less talent were going for ridiculous amounts so Kamara pushed the deal through straight away. He thought he was getting a bargain. So did I. Silky did the deal, and I was very grateful for the money I started on. Five years previously I had been allowed £20 a week.

The first training run was the hardest of my life. I'd been pissing it up for weeks in Jamaica and those five-and-a-half miles with Kamara were murder. Me and Nicky Mohan, who I knew from Leicester, stayed at the back. A very fit Kamara was leading from the front. I soon realised it was a proper running club, which suited me. Within ten days I quickly got fit again, was able to keep up and winning the power running over shorter distances. Kamara was a little eccentric and had some funny ideas about training. Like we had to do one-on-one training, not on a portion of the pitch, which is normal, but full length. That's never been known before and it was exhausting. At least we got really, really fit.

Kamara was a much-travelled midfielder in his playing days. He's now a football analyst on Sky Sports and an after-dinner speaker; well respected, though his comments are sometimes off-key. A typical combative, never-say-die midfielder on his travels, his best days were in the eighties with teams like Swindon Town, Portsmouth, Brentford, Leeds United and Stoke City. A Lionel Richie look-alike, he's retained that eighties look, too, with the gheri-curl hair and pencil-thin moustache. No wonder he does a mean version of Richie's 'Dancing On The Ceiling' on the karaoke machine.

For all his keenness to sign me, I did not impress straight away. Kamara felt I was performing in spasms for only ten minutes at a time in a game. He was not happy and must have rued the day he bought me. Kamara knew I was a ladies man. He said I needed to control myself better. At the same time as me he bought Peter Beagrie from Manchester City for the same amount and got the same effort. Kamara noticed I was not vocal in the dressing room, but took a lot of what he said onto the pitch. He liked it that I was prepared to follow his instructions.

Kamara felt I was an absolute certainty to be a Jamaican international. Even though Jamaica never had the luxury of top class Premiership players, he felt they were a good option for players like me and Robbie Earle, who played at top club level but were overlooked by England. I'm not saying I was good enough to play for England but when you see some of the players they have picked for international duty over the years, you wonder what the criteria are.

Craig Ramage (Ram), the ex-England Under-21 player, joined Bradford at the same time as me in 1997 as did Darren Moore, a big black defender who had come from Doncaster. He was a funny white geezer, Ram signed from Watford. Being new, we stuck together. On the first day we were in a car going to training and he said to Darren, 'What's happening, brothers. Yeah, cool bro. You know, Darren, I've got more black friends than you.' We were stunned; didn't know how to take him, but then we creased up. Ram thinks he's ghetto heaven. Only he could start talking 'black' to two black strangers and not get beaten up.

Wayne Jacobs is another great mate from my Bradford days. He is a left back and a very quiet, Christian man. At the time of writing assistant manager of Halifax Town, I think he has a lot of the qualities needed to go a long way as a manager. Wayne wasn't a socialite and has a very calming nature (the total opposite to me). Yet there was a mutual respect. He admired the fact I was a fantastic trainer and was always full on, even in training. I never held anything back. Wayne said he would always have me in the trenches with him and was amused that, despite my toughness, I was always getting injured – me and Mooro, the giant black defender. They would have bets on which of the two of us would be first to the physios.

Wayne thinks I would be good at mentoring kids. In prison I didn't waste my time. I read a lot and got a distinction in maths and my City and Guilds Certificate in Car Mechanics.

Another character was Eddie Youds, who joined in 1997. Liverpudlian, he has a typical Scouser's sense of humour. Eddie grew up in Ipswich. During pre-season training he got to know us by socialising. He liked the fact that I could look after myself and he joked that I was the first black man he'd ever met who drank Guinness heavy. Eddie teased me that I liked the girls, but they were never the best-looking. I was a bit of a gentleman. He claimed I was the second-best looking player in the club.

Youds thinks all the fans liked me because I played with my heart on my sleeve and was prepared to run through brick walls. He rated me as the biggest team player there, prepared to do anything to make the team better. On the pitch I was a manager's dream, but away from it, Eddie thought I was a manager's nightmare. He respected Bradford for giving me a chance, felt it made me a stronger, better person, and was really pleased for me when my Jamaica call-up came. If I was hyper before, I was even more full of life then.

Peter Beagrie (Beags) felt we had one of the best team spirits of any club he played for. He should know: he was an England international and was at Manchester City and Everton. We were a close-knit bunch at Bradford. Peter was one of the stalwarts and we surprised everyone when we got promoted to the Prem after a bad start. Beags felt our success was down to how well we gelled despite our diverse backgrounds and saw me as the pivotal player. He played on the wing – usually left – and I played just inside. If the other side had a star man, I was stuck on him, which was good for Beags, who had 'happy feet'. We had a four-four-two shape that we stuck to rigidly and anyone coming in it was like-for-like. The level of performance demanded that we were always on top of our game, no egos. I got on brilliantly with Beags. He introduced me to Laurent Perrier pink champagne, one of the few non-Guinness drinks I like. We also shared the love of the gym. Beags teased me about my muscular torso and ridiculously skinny legs, but couldn't believe they ran like the wind. He thought it was hilarious that I spent more time with the physio than on the pitch, partly because I threw myself into tackles. 'Jamie, if we had a fight I would hit you, but you would tackle me.' Beags is a player-coach at Scunthorpe and, with his great footballing brain, I think he can go a long way.

He laughed when I was featured in the *Daily Sport* under the headline: 'Footballer With An Eleven-Inch Willy.' Then they ran the story again, only it was even more flattering: 'Footballer With A Twelve-Inch Willy.' 'With an appendage like that you could use it as a skipping rope,' Beags said. 'Or a fishing rod. No wonder you live life to the full!'

He used to tease me about my hair, but I said, 'I haven't got happy feet like you, Beags, but this will get me headlines.' He couldn't believe how much I was spending on designer clothes. Prada was my favourite at the time. Taxi fares, too – I would think nothing of spending £300 on a Monday morning taxi from London to training in Bradford. I would text or phone him to request a heavy session in the gym so I could sweat out all the weekend's excesses. Beags knew that no matter how hard I partied, in a mid-week match or Saturday game I would be ready. That's where Paul Jewell's man-management skills showed: he allowed me a lot of leeway because I never let him down in a match. I gave him powerhouse performances and Beags remembers a couple of stunning goals against West Ham and one that started on the halfway line against Norwich. He joked that I even matched his skills on occasions. Beags also remembers my headlocks as being the hardest to escape from.

Darren Moore signed from Doncaster for £175,000. We hit it off straight away and have been in contact ever since. Darren had heard I was quick, but says he didn't realise just how fast I could be. He played for Jamaica too, against Panama, Romania and Canada and a couple of other games. I was well respected in Jamaica. I got my head down and the coaches loved me for my work ethic. They took me off the wings and liked to play me in more central midfield.

Darren felt he never went out for a quiet drink with me, more an event. He warned a new player, Steve McNespie, who was on loan from Fulham, not to try to compete with me and told him if he was going out with me to pace himself. Macho egos dominate footballers' mindsets and McNespie could not resist the challenge. He tried to go one-to-one with me throughout the night. Big mistake! Next day at training I had a big grin on my face. Fresh as a daisy, I was the first one at training as usual, raring to go. There was no sign of Steve. Darren was worried and went to his hotel. He persuaded the staff to let him go in to check on Steve and found the poor guy unconscious in his bed, having lost control of all his bodily functions. But the next day he managed to get to training and said to Darren, 'I don't know why I didn't listen to you.' We had a good laugh about it.

Mooro's most memorable game was that heart-stopper for promotion to the Prem against Wolves in May 1999. He remembers a challenge I made in the first two minutes that set the tone for the rest of the game. It was a match of incredible excitement and he reckons that game cemented the Bradford fans' love

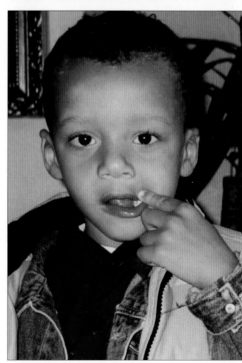

Top left: My mum Elfreda.

Top right: With my dad Dudley.

Bottom left: With Tiagh.

Bottom right: With Nathan.

Top: Cleaning my football boots in my Camp Hill prison cell. The desk in the corner is where I'd write love letters to various lucky ladies.   © *Solo Syndication*

Bottom left: With my sister Val.

Bottom right: Looking slick, rude-boy style in Battersea, aged seventeen.

Top: Shorty Malcolm's funeral was a massive event in Jamaica with (*bottom*) the Boyz all present to pay our respects.

Top left: With my mate Gee.

Top right: With Ricardo Fuller living it up after a hard day's training with the Jamaica team in Miami.

The loves of my life, (*left*) Rowena and (*above*) Guinness.

for me. But at first things were not great. 'This is a big, massive mistake,' I thought when I first arrived at Bradford and wanted to get on the next train home. But the people made me feel welcome and the players liked my one hundred per cent commitment. Gary Walsh, Peter Beagrie and Mark Prudhoe were also new to the club. We were all signed at once and became the nucleus.

* * * * *

Keen to make an impression, on and off the pitch, I got into the party scene quick. I was on it regular like clockwork. There was a ladies' night at the Park Pub, where girls drank free all night. I was definitely turning up for that one. One chick I liked was Carlie. She was a stunner, beautiful skin with a nice pair of breasts. The way she carried herself all the lads wanted her. But every time I tried to talk to her, she sent me down the river, blanked all the time.

* * * * *

I played in the first game of the 97-98 season against Stockport County at home. I played well and got a good reception from the fans, which helped me settle. We won 2-1. At first we did well, winning four and drawing the other in our first five matches. We were flying. Everyone was expecting big things. In our fourth league game I scored my first goal for the club, away to Reading: a header. We won 3-0, moved up to second place and thought this was going to be the year we turned things around. It was a good run early doors and my form was good, but I wasn't consistent.

Then we dropped off; I'm not sure why. It started with a 4-0 thrashing at Sunderland. I was still raw and not used to the physical demands in the pro game, and it showed, unlike Doncaster, who were in the old Third Division. Now I was playing better players all round and my body was getting tired. Perhaps it didn't help that I was living fast and burning candles at both ends. It was not long after jail and I was still trying to catch up on lost time. Team-mates Robbie Blake, Lawrence Davies and David Donaldson used to stay at my house regularly. We partied hardcore and I knew we were off-key, but we still got on with everyone. There was no one at the club that I didn't like.

As we lost our form we really started struggling, dropping from top spot in September to thirteenth by November. Kamara was alright as a manager, but he wasn't getting the results, losing the confidence of the players and, by the New Year, things looked ominous...

* * * * *

I had a Beemer, a 3.20 convertible, then – bought it off my mate, Nicky for £10,000 cash. Thought it was the bollocks. Chicks were on me, man. I had the pineapple, so it wasn't hard to pick me out. Life was so sweet in those early days at Valley Parade. One lovely summer's day I came down from Bradford and went to watch football at The Crown in Battersea with Dean Johns.

We went for a drive in the new convertible and these guys were walking into a chip shop. Envious, they gave us the wanker's sign. We passed them, went round the block and pulled up outside the chippie. One of the guys pointed at his mate blaming him. We walked in there and just as it was about to go off the police turned up. They searched all of us and found a ball of puff no bigger than a rabbit's dropping in one of the guys' pockets. 'You're nicking me for that!' He couldn't believe it. Laughing, we went in the pub to watch the football.

For the first three months I was staying in the Holiday Inn Hotel before buying a house in Leeds for £84,000 with a five per cent deposit. I moved in a month later. It was a new-build three-bed, three toilets, one en-suite, garage, front and back garden. For that money you couldn't go wrong. I wanted to get on the property ladder straight away. It made sense 'cos I was earning good dough and Leeds was a boomtown. Turned out to be a good purchase because it has doubled in value...

Some of us were indulging in some hardcore partying in those early days; some of it was really off-key. To show how bad we were, Robbie Blake must have gone drinking on a Saturday night and was still drunk the next day. He bet us that he could get to 80mph in a 30mph speed zone. Pulled up by the police, he tried to pretend he was sober. But Blakey was so drunk he fell over his feet as he got out and was arrested for drink-driving. At the next game there was no sign of him. He was dropped, but the manager didn't say anything. Another time Craig Midgley and Ram got into a fight with some bouncers at a nightclub. Ram's tear duct was damaged as he took a bashing whilst Midge was running away. Good thing Ram lived miles away in Derby, otherwise he would have come off much worse!

By Christmas 1997 we had dropped off so badly that Kamara, sensing the inevitable, sat us down for a big, serious meeting to ask why, then went through the whole team one by one. My reputation for partying was already big. Everything was solemn and tense until he got to me. 'And you, with your mustard-coloured eyes, I don't know what I'm gonna get out of you.' We cracked up. My partying was affecting my football even though I couldn't admit it at the time. From that day I was a model player.

In January 1998 Kamara was sacked. We felt it was a bit harsh because the team had a lot of new players who were taking some time to gel. His assistant, Paul Jewell, took over for the rest of the season and didn't do much better, but under the circumstances it was far from easy. Jewell was a former Bradford player with nearly 400 games behind him so there was a feeling that everything he was trying to do was for love and he desperately wanted the club to succeed. Being only thirty-three didn't help. Jewell was probably the youngest manager in the league and obviously needed time to learn his craft properly. There were even players older than him so it was a tough baptism and touch and go whether or not he would pull through.

* * * * *

When Gareth Grant signed in 1997 he was on the Youth Training Scheme and assigned to be my boot boy. There weren't many black players and as he was from Leeds he showed me around. I took him under my wing. He was only earning £42 a week, so when we went out, I would treat him. Gareth introduced me to the designer shop Flannels in Leeds, where I'd buy up all the Dolce & Gabbana and Prada. I used to buy black trousers by the truckload. Some I never wore and just kept them in the wrapping. The average price was £150 a pop. Gareth insisted they all looked the same, but only I knew the subtle differences between each pair. Sometimes I'd give him a brand new pair. He was very grateful, a nice kid. Everything got dry-cleaned after only one wearing. Keeping up an image was very costly. The cleaning bills alone were about £100 a week.

At least it helped attracting the girls. The actress Samantha Janus took an interest one night in a bar. Lot of flirting, but nothing happened. It boosted my ego, though. When you go out and dress up to the nines and make a proper effort, unexpected things can happen. My style was Mafia-style long jackets, smart shoes and trousers. Rarely casual, I was proper t'ings.

At the time I was changing girlfriends like underwear. Gareth was well amused. Every week it seemed I had found the love of my life and got engaged. He reckons I was getting engaged after twenty-four hours of meeting a girl, telling him I'd found my soul-mate and to get ready for a wedding. I'd be so happy in the honeymoon period, then it would fizzle out just as quickly as it started.

That first Christmas at Bradford Gareth was drinking with us in the Square On The Lane bar and moaning that he had to leave early for a boring club function. Being a senior player, I was allowed to miss it. A few hours later Gareth returned to find me in one of the alcoves dancing butt naked with the Leeds United players Gary Kelly and Jonathan Woodgate egging me on. It's amazing how uninhibited gallons of Guinness can make you. Kelly is Irish and he said he's never seen anyone drink so much of the black stuff. The barmen got into the spirit and laughed before I put my clothes back on. I only did it because the Leeds lads had heard about my package and were curious to see it. Gareth said the girls called it the Loch Ness Monster.

A few years later I had a stud inserted. The piercing is supposed to heighten a woman's pleasure on her G-spot. It was uncomfortable for the first two weeks, bleeding for three weeks and the doctors said I shouldn't have sex, nor do any physical activity for a while, but I still had to train and running was a bit painful. Later, when I moved to Brentford and they saw it in the showers, someone asked, 'What the fuck is that?' It became an exhibit.

I realised I had something special after sex with my first two partners. The first one kept on coming back for more and I know it wasn't my technique. When the second one saw it for the first time, she exclaimed, 'Fucking hell, this is big!' In those days my philosophy was every hole's a goal. No wonder I got in the *Daily Sport* with stories like 'Footballer With Eleven-Inch Willy' and 'Footballer with Twelve-Inch Willy'. I got even more girls after that.

Gareth was not only surprised that I was still standing at the end of the night, but able to eat my regular fried chicken and chips from the local takeaway. He knew I missed London a lot and partying was my way of dealing with the loneliness. But he couldn't believe how fresh and ready for action I always was the morning after a session – must be great genes. One night I got a girl back to my hotel room and told Gareth to come in to take over after I'd finished. He sneaked in whilst I was doing the business and sat waiting for his turn. When I'd finished the girl was eager for more and I looked over at Gareth, but he had fallen asleep.

It was around that time I set my record for continuous pints of Guinness. The sessions after Tuesday training were the best 'cos we usually had Wednesdays off. So it was an excuse to let off completely. Over a twelve-hour period from 2pm I downed pint after pint. We started in a pub, then a restaurant, then finished at a club in the early hours. Thirty-two pints! Hard to believe, but in the morning I felt alright. I got props from my mates. Northerners often think we Southerners are softies and can't drink, especially black men who only sip Jack Daniels and coke, but I proved myself that night.

At the time the centre-half Eddie Youds was a good mate of Paul Jewell and, after an away match, I went with Eddie for a drink. We met up with Jewell, who was still No.2 at Bradford. It was the first time I'd spoken to Paul properly and the start of a friendship that's still strong today.

In Bradford there was a lap-dancing club with a great name: DV8. When I first arrived at the club I went in there a few times, mainly out of boredom. After a while a hotel room can seem like a prison cell and there was no way I wanted to repeat that experience. One of the dancers took a shine to me, so I got her number and arranged for a future rendezvous. She was game for anything. Back at my hotel room I set up a camera and decided to make my own film. She was playing with herself and I was zooming in. Then I introduced two bottles of champagne and placed them strategically around her body, and then some... When I showed it to the boys, they thought my package was the Loch Ness Monster come to town. She was happy with her movie debut – she felt like a star. Kamara allowed a player to use his office to watch what he thought was a football video. When he returned from training about ten players were crammed into his room. Three guesses of what they were watching. He shooed them out, but I bet he had a sly look at it before I got it back.

Eddie Youds thought my film was hilarious. He told me everyone in the club saw it, even the canteen ladies. Eddie saw it before a training session and said it was a lovely start to the day. He also said she was a looker – for a change. After a while I smashed up the tape so it wouldn't come back to haunt me.

We finished the 1997–98 season in thirteenth place, losing four of the last five matches and drawing the other. Paul Jewell was under intense pressure and a lot of people wanted him out. Youds got sold with a couple of others. I thought we would struggle to stay together, but Jewell was given a few million to spend by the chairman Geoffrey Richmond and he invested well. Gareth Whalley, Isaiah Rankin, Ashley Westwood, Lee Mills all came in that summer and Stuart McCall returned. Teams don't gel straight away, but I vowed to myself I would be at my best to help the cause and would be back fit. This was a crossroads in my career and I didn't want to waste it. Little did I know an injury was to put my whole career in jeopardy.

Chapter 12

PERK OF THE JOB

Young men with athletic physiques, plenty of cash, lots of time on their hands and a very high level of testosterone coursing through their bodies are likely to have only one thing on their minds. Only Guinness comes close to having sex – and then it's a distant second. I'm lucky enough to be in a settled relationship with my partner Rowena and our daughter Tiagh, but before that I unashamedly admit I used to love bit of pussy. I saw it as a necessity of a footballer's life, a welcome stress buster after the pressure of performing before crowds of thousands and TV audiences of millions. Sex is great whether you're elated after a win or depressed after a loss. If you're injured it can help take your mind off not playing and when you're playing well, it is the perfect complement to make you feel even better than you already do. Remember, I've never smoked a cigarette or touched any drugs. Nor do I gamble. A man's got to have some vices. Anyway, any self-respecting player always analyses his game after a match. The adrenaline is still pumping hours later and a man can climb walls breaking down the game. We deserve a release like anyone else.

I've already mentioned Miss X. She was wild. We were rampant: hot, sweaty, raw sex, proper. I used to see her in raves and always fancied her. Then I saw her at SW1 club in Victoria. She was on a first date with a brother, but I chirpsed [charmed] her away. She was gorgeous: brown hair, nice tan, silicone stand-up breasts, about 5ft 4in with a black-girl's bottom. Proper bumper, bare low tops. What an exhibitionist! We couldn't keep our hands off each other after that first night. One time she started blowing me in the back of my mate's car. When the driver noticed he got excited and thought his turn was next. Miss X looked up and said, 'Don't you fucking think about it!' She's hot, but likes her t'ings so much if we had had an exclusive relationship I'd have had to put an electronic tag on her to make sure the next man don't go there. Just to show you how hot she was she later won a competition in a famous lads mag.

The Coliseum in Vauxhall has happy memories too. One July evening I went out with my girlfriend at the time and while I was there I pulled another girl. Would you believe another busty blonde? She looked at me in the club and I knew it was on. Whilst my girl was being entertained by Speller and the rest of our crowd, I took her outside to her car and did it there and then. She just wanted a good time and who was I to deny her that pleasure? I took my girl home and got a blow-job before I had time to have a wash.

I rang the latest conquest up soon afterwards. She lived in Slough, a few miles west of Heathrow Airport, about thirty miles from me. She would drive over and I knew a little side road beside Battersea Dogs Home where I could bang her on the bonnet. Great fun! That's all we were having, fun. I knew she weren't going to be my wife. It was about the time Lesley first got pregnant and I'd moved in with Tasha.

At Bradford a buff girl worked in the Heartbeat Gym in the city centre. The players had free access. All the man dem fancied her. Brown hair, tanned, slim, shapely, she worked out all the time – and it showed. Fit! She loved a night out, too and enjoyed a drink. Great sense of humour and very sexy. I found out she didn't have a man and sent her flowers. She came to a game and I took her out after. I couldn't keep my hands off her that night. Good grind! Done her a few times after. I'd finally broken my duck in Bradford. Up till then I was only interested in London girls. Every opportunity back then I went home to London. She became a regular item for a while. She started leaving her door open for me to come round and shag her. She was fiery and sometimes we both ended up sore. It was a convenient arrangement because she wasn't looking for a relationship.

Another Bradford lass who tempted me to stay a few times was one of the girls who worked in the players' bar. Blonde, big tits, all the attributes a quality barmaid should have. I'd chat to her and she made me wait a while. Nuff man hit on her, but she liked the Lawrence. One night after a game I ended up having her. A day that sticks out them times was when I got two bottles of champagne for being Man of the Match. I drunk them with my mates, then went back to her house to bang her. It lasted over a year but we had to split because she was falling in love with me. That didn't stop us from getting together one more time a year later, though.

* * * * *

Ayia Napa is a popular place for single men. I used to go regularly. Years before I met Rowena I was there one afternoon with some team-mates on the beach and I got chatting to a girl. Two-twos, I started feeling tusky and wanted to take her back to my room. I left the door ajar for my mates to watch, and they did. We did the business and parted. That night a well-known footballer pulled the same girl and went down on her. He is a Premiership player and still playing now. They were at it pretty heavy, but she wouldn't go all the way. She told us so word got around. He still gets teased to this day.

I've been featured in some newspaper articles, too. Kiss-and-tell stories are all part of the territory, especially when you're a Premiership player. That quality paper the *Sunday Sport* did an 'exposé' on me years ago. The headline was very flattering: 'Premiership Ace's 10-Incher Hurt But I Begged Him Not To Stop...' It made for X-rated reading, too:

Premier League wildman Jamie Lawrence enjoyed a blow-job while he boasted on the phone to a pal how he was joining Sheffield Wednesday to double his money. The cheeky call was made from a London hotel room where Jamie and Emma Parris later had sex in four different positions.

And when the Bradford winger stripped naked, sales executive Emma trembled with fear. The mousey-haired Londoner, 25, said: 'It was huge. I reckon it was about ten inches and I thought 'no fucking way'. I really didn't know if I could take that much. It was quite thick too. Emma added: 'That's going to do some damage. I didn't even think the condom would go on. But I was looking forward to it because I'd heard rumours about it. The first thing I did was give him a blow-job and I could hardly get it in my mouth...'

The article goes on to describe in graphic detail what happened next. I took a lot of ribbing from my team-mates, but it's hardly something to be ashamed of, is it? Andy Myers says my dick is like a baby's arm. 'You're not shy to get out your weapon, are you, Jamie?' he used to say. 'When you got it out, the girls would either run a mile or stay out of intrigue.'

Looking back on the whole episode I realise it was a total set-up. It started with a text from nowhere on my mobile: 'I want it hard and deep.' Obviously a set-up, but the lust and curiosity was killing me. I texted back: 'Who the fuck is this?' She texted me where to meet her in Wimbledon. My mate Gee picked me up. Alarm bells were ringing all over the place. Dad had just died, I was still feeling low and even if it was a trap, I didn't think the publicity would be bad. She insisted on paying for the hotel, bought all the drinks. I thought it was the man who was supposed to get the girls drunk and take advantage! When we came out of the hotel Gee picked me up and we both agreed that this was a classic kiss-and-tell situation. Sure enough, the story appeared soon after.

When I first started playing for Jamaica in summer 2000 I socialised with Deon Burton. One night we were in a London nightclub and he bumped into a girl he'd had a fling with in Ayia Napa. We ended up in her house and I was with her mate. That was a wild night – Deon's girl was a porn star. The night started with her showing us one of her films, which set the tone beautifully for the action afterwards. I started in a room with my one and the other girl was in another bedroom with Deon. We could hear each other so it was a natural progression for me to suggest we should all get together in one room. That's when they started getting freaky. We ended up shagging both of them and they even put on a lesbian show for us. It went on all night. Both were blondes, one had fake titties and they loved men and women in equal measure.

Soon after that I met Rowena and was immediately attracted to her because she was a challenge. Not only was she very attractive but she acted stush [superior], like she never wanted anyone to talk to her. She made me work hard to woo her, but she was certainly worth it.

* * * * *

Professional football is not all fun and glamour. So many people are hungry to make it that they will dedicate themselves 24-7 to achieve that. A typical Saturday match's preparation starts on a Friday when we train. Not always light either, sometimes we have a good blow. There is a curfew from the Thursday night. Friday night you chill and eat plenty of pasta and drink lots of water. Living right is very important. I'm a very early riser on a match day and have a full English breakfast as soon as I get up. A lot of players have a light pre-match meal around 11.45am, but I don't eat again.

On match days my missus can't talk to me because I'm all wound up. I snap at her and I'm very tetchy. I get to the ground between 1 and 1.30pm then we get changed and prepare. We have a team talk and the manager tells you about the opposition. Some players may need strapping by the physio. Around 2.15 we go onto the pitch to warm up, come back into the dressing room, then go out around 2.55. We shake hands with the opposition then go to war. I've never felt like not playing, the adrenaline is too great.

After the match you might go for a drink in the players' lounge if you know any of the opposition, but in the nineties some clubs started moving away from the drinking culture and stopped providing alcohol to the players so we would arrange to meet in a pub nearby. Despite public perception, most players respect themselves as professional athletes. Virtually everyone enjoys a drink and few have a real problem. Considering how much money they have, players generally are quite well behaved. Occasional brawls are blown up out of proportion and the papers love to exaggerate them. In thousands of pubs and clubs ordinary Joe Bloggs are fighting, but that's not reported. Most of those ordinary guys start on footballers, wanting to provoke them so they can cash in by selling the story to the papers.

Group sex (or 'roasting') happens, but I'm not being funny, which red-blooded young man, even old man for that matter, wouldn't go for casual sex if the girl's willing and able? Rape accusations are usually the girls trying to cash in. I think they're the ones who should be locked up – they're trying to mash up homes and careers.

I've never seen a drug culture, performance enhancing or leisure, at any of the clubs I played for. I hate being around ganja smokers, but at least it's the lesser of the evils. Some players may pop pills and snort coke, but I've never come across anyone who does – they've got too much to lose. Puffing hurts people and they get paranoid and off-key. I've seen people smoking, even dealers who are selling ganja who take a little piece for personal use, then it's a medium piece, and before they know it, they're hooked and taking gear like there's no tomorrow. Tony Montana's experience in *Scarface* is a strong reminder not to get high on your own supply. He is loose-balling at the end, with no control of the drugs, nor the dealers or where his money's at.

* * * * *

When I wasn't chasing pussy, I watched lots of DVDs. Favourites are hardcore gangster classics like *Scarface*, *Goodfellas*, *Harder They Come*, *The Godfather*, *Heat*, *Missippi Burning* (which really touched me) and *John Q*, where Denzel Washington's son needs a heart transplant but he doesn't have medical insurance. Denzel's willing to give his own life to save his son and

I can identify with that. Denzel is heavy. I admire De Niro, Pacino, Brando and Samuel L Jackson, and Halle Berry would be my fantasy wife.

My music tastes are the bashment type of reggae. Artists like Super Cat, Ninja Man and the legends like Bob Marley, Gregory 'Cool Ruler' Isaacs and Dennis Brown. Sunday in our house was music day when Dad used to play his records. I also like rare groove and R'n'B. When Jamaicans first came to Britain they used to organise 'shabeens' (unlicensed clubs) because the regular pubs and clubs were too racist. They died out in the eighties, but I went to a wicked one in Bradford. People used to look out for me there because there were a lot of low-life characters. It was called Planet Venus and most of the women were prostitutes.

As a footballer there are many boring hours spent sitting around trying to conserve your energy, so watching TV is all part of the life. My favourite shows are *The Sopranos* and *The Shield*. I always buy the DVD series packs because I hate missing Tony Soprano's gangster ways. He keeps it real, blood. Even though he's racist and wicked, he's a proper businessman. *24* is interesting, too. I've been known to watch it on DVD for twenty hours straight. I find it fascinating. In *24* certain things that we don't realise go on and information that does not reach the people is revealed. I introduced Andy Myers to it.

This may sound funny coming from me, but I watch all the soaps. When I was up North, I had nuff time on my hands and they kept me going early evening. It was my route to 9pm. First, *Neighbours*, then *Home and Away*, *Family Affairs*, *Emmerdale*, then *Coronation Street* or *EastEnders*, and sometimes *The Bill*. I never used to watch *The Bill* but it's heavy now because they don't always solve the case in one episode. Sometimes it takes them three or four episodes, or it even goes on for weeks. To me, it's more real because they don't nick all the criminals every time.

I also play a lot of computer games to ease the boredom: 'Hitman', 'Contract Killing', 'Grand Theft Auto'. I can be on 'Auto' until 4am. I've got a Game Boy, which I bought in Jamaica, and a Pacman helps pass the time – I've got heavy on Pacman.

My favourite sportsmen are Mike Tyson and John Barnes, who was the first black man after Howard Gayle to establish himself in the Liverpool side. Barnes tore it up. The West Indian cricketers Michael 'Whispering Death' Holding, Viv Richards and Courtney Walsh are also sportsmen I admire. I went to Walsh's sports bar in Kingston with a couple of Reggae Boyz and he really looked after us – real gentleman. I preferred Marvin Hagler to Sugar Ray Leonard: Hagler came from the ghetto and kept it real.

Chapter 13

KEEPING WOLVES AT BAY

Two days before Bradford were going to St Kitts in the Caribbean on our 1998 club tour I pulled a hamstring. St Kitts is one of those tiny, unspoilt islands that you never want to leave. It is relatively wealthy so the standard of living is high and I was really looking forward to it. Not going really cut me up. Paul Jewell told me to go to the physio while they were away. Steve Redman, the club physio, had booked me into a rehab clinic and he used to phone up to see how my injury was repairing. The clinic said that Stuart 'Macca' McCall had been coming in for treatment but Jamie Lawrence was nowhere to be seen. Somehow, the rumour got back to Jewell that I'd been seen in Ayia Napa dancing on a balcony. Someone also sent in a letter saying that they'd seen me out there. I actually went twice because I'd met this Cypriot girl, Kelly. Long hair, green eyes... Done up she looked wicked and she was hot in bed, man. Nine-and-a-half out of ten!

Spoony the dj was in Ayia Napa at the same time. He's a fit man who doesn't drink and mentioned to me that he fancied a work out. We were chillin' together on the beach and I suggested we go to the gym. Spoony wanted a heavy session, and that's when my competitive nature kicked in. I worked him so hard, the next day he said, 'Jamie, that's the nearest a person can get to legally killing me. I'm so sore it's a joke. Good job the hot weather is helping my muscles to recover.' Spoony is a proper piss-taker. He says, 'You may have a big dick but whether you can use it properly is debatable. I reckon it's just for show, like a museum piece.' Whatever.

When he got back Jewell pulled me in and asked if it was true. He threatened to fine me two weeks' wages and put me on the transfer list if I didn't tell the truth. I just told him I couldn't stand the thought of everybody being in St Kitts when I was stuck in cold, rainy, grey Yorkshire and I only went for a few days. 'Anyway, gaffer,' I smiled. 'It turned out cool because I met a girl out there and the heat, champagne and sex did the trick on my leg.' Jewell was so amused he didn't punish me – he knew I was a true team-man.

There was no holiday that summer, no drinking even. Tasha thought I was a nutter because of the way I determined to get fit. I was running twice a day, sometimes at one in the morning, and timing everything trying to get faster. A black man running in the middle of the night must have created some suspicions, but getting in the best shape of my life was so important. It paid off straight away. I was fourth fastest in the long-distance running and cleaned up on the power running. Pissing it, in fact. Jewell was impressed. He said, 'You've come back tremendously well and in great shape and I'm giving you a four-year contract.' It was music to my ears.

To hone our fitness, he took us to an army camp. John McGinlay, a cheeky Scottish forward who had seen it all in the game as he approached retirement, was in the squad. What a character! He didn't give a fuck. Four of us were drinking in someone's room but it was after the midnight curfew. We knew Jewell patrolled the corridors so had to be careful. Two of us were in the grounds going back to our rooms with two behind. We heard Jewell catch them but we jumped through the windows into our rooms just in time. The next morning they got £500 fines. Jewell accused McGinlay of being out with us. He had broken the curfew, but not with us. McGinlay claimed when Jewell was knocking on his door, he was fast asleep and couldn't hear him. 'I don't believe you,' Jewell said. 'Prove it!' McGinlay laughed.

The 1998–99 season started badly. Our opening match was a 2-1 loss at home to Stockport, then we lost at Watford, drew with Bolton, lost at Crewe and finally beat Birmingham at home 2-1 for our first league win of the season. There was a strong call for Jewell's head and his sacking looked certain. But somehow something just clicked after that and we rarely lost. Even when we were losing we somehow managed to pull out a victory. Team spirit was tremendous. At the start of that run I damaged my knee in the Birmingham game and was out for four weeks. Sunderland were runaway leaders and the chase was on with Ipswich for the other automatic place.

Along the way we bought Dean Windass and Lee Sharpe, who strengthened the side. Sharpe, a tricky left-winger, had won nuff things with Man United and played eight times for England so he was a good addition. As for Windass, my spirit didn't take to him and the reason why soon became clear...

Boxers like to train in the most atrocious, Spartan gyms because it builds up their toughness. Bradford City must have adopted that philosophy because their training ground, at Apperley Bridge, was as horrible as they come. It was always muddy, especially when it rained and mixed with sewage when the river overflowed. Some players – like Sharpey who was used to the luxury of Man United facilities – complained, but after life in jail it didn't bother me. There were no shower facilities at Apperley Bridge so you had to get into your kriss [immaculate] car in filthy gear at the end of a session. It pissed us off in the winter, but it kept everyone grounded. People coming from bigger clubs called Bradford the Dog and Duck pub side but having been at Leicester and Sunderland where the training facilities are better, it still didn't bother me. The weights room was shit, too – there weren't enough of them so we just made the best of what we had. For me it was paradise after what I'd been through.

Beags, a larger-than-life character, was a cool guy, but Sharpey didn't really get on with him, partly because they were in the same position.

During that run I scored my best goal ever, at home against Norwich in April 1998. From the halfway line I beat three or four before smashing it home. I also won a penalty in a 4-1 victory. It was one of those games where absolutely everything seemed to go right. Even when I mis-hit a pass it turned out to be a brilliant ball to someone else. Needless to say, I got the Man of the Match award.

Gaffer helped keep the team spirit going by taking us out once a month. They were tremendous bonding sessions. Paul Jewell was a brave man! I was at the peak of my fitness and drinking less. By now my body could stand up to playing two matches a week. I had a little drop in form, but was playing well enough. I was seen as the hard-working, industrious right midfielder with Beags on the wing for his skill and trickery. There was balance and quality in that side and everyone knew what they were doing. The money was good, too. Bonuses were £1,200 and, as we were playing up to eight times a month, I felt blessed. After training I used to shop a lot with Isaiah. I was living right and life felt good. There were nuff girls, including Carlie, the Halle Berry lookalike, who I chased for eighteen months. Life was nice; everything was blessed.

My mates used to come up from London to keep me company. One of them was Reds. We'd grown up together and are still close now. Reds was a sly kid. As a thirteen-year-old he nicked £450 raffle ticket money from the Dunston Community Centre. Being from Brixton he was able to disappear awhile and enjoy his windfall. Reds was at Feltham and Dover with me. He reckons as teenagers Ray and I styled ourselves as the Krays and our Firm were all the bad boy white kids.

Reds met some girls in Bradford City centre one night in March 1999 and brought them to my Leeds house in his Jeep. Two-twos we all paired off and retired to bed. Reds heard my girl say, 'Cor blimey, he's got one down to his knees! I think it's the Yorkshire Ripper!' In the morning Reds and our mate Titch were in the spare bedroom with their girls and I came to the doorway butt-naked. 'Fuck off, James, they won't want us no more now!' Reds said. Great times.

One incident wasn't great, though. A girl came back to the house, got blind drunk and started screaming the street down in the early hours of Sunday morning. She was getting hysterical for nothing, a big drama in a posh area. It was embarrassing. We eventually managed to push her into a taxi.

One wicked night in London with Reds we went to the Astoria in the West End for the Radio One Dream Team's birthday party. Reds and Titch challenged me to a drinking contest and were cheating, but I didn't realise. I got wankered! They really messed me up. DJ Spoony suddenly announced, 'Jamie's got his monster out!' At the time I'd do anything for publicity, which is partly why I'd dyed my hair all crazy colours. It could help me get a move.

At the Coliseum in Vauxhall another night some guys were getting lairy. Giving it a bit. I moved towards them, saying, 'I'll fucking knock you out!' When they realised who I was with – Reds, Titch, Speller and the rest – they backed off.

* * * * *

Many amateur players think that with the right breaks they could have made it as a pro. Reds is one of them. He used to run a five-a-side team in Croydon. Ray was in the team. I went down to watch when they were a man short. With my dyed hair and relative fame from playing for Bradford it was hard not to spot me. Reds gave me some kit and told me to take it easy. The opposition complained that I was a ringer but I played anyway. At the end of the match, the ref shook Reds's hand and congratulated him on being the Man of the Match. 'See Jamie, you know you're not ready. You can't trap a bag of sand.' When that happened a second time, with the ref shaking Reds's hand, he said, 'Paul Jewell is going to put me in the team and you on the bench.' Reds has always had delusions of being a pro.

Throughout my time at Bradford Steve Redman, the physio, used to say, 'I'm glad I'm treating you, Jamie, and not the people you hit.' Wingers are generally not very physical players and a fullback can often intimidate them. One whack and the winger usually loses his arsehole – but not me. Redders said, 'You can tackle a good fullback. They can't relish facing you, Jamie.' He was amused that I never went to him with the run-of-the-mill stuff like groin strains, back twinges and pulled muscles. When I saw Redders it was for a proper injury, like broken bones. Fingers, thumbs, ankles, ribs... I broke them all. At least I hadn't broken a leg. Well, not yet anyway. I broke my cheekbone once and had to wear a protective mask for a month like Paul Gascoigne and Gary Lineker. Redders was impressed that I was playing again within ten days, which was very unusual for that kind of injury.

Being a whole-hearted player the desire to give one hundred per cent put me in scrapes, but I was never a dirty player. That's never been the spirit I've competed in. If I can't win (reasonably) fairly, then I don't want to win at all. When the manager wanted steel in midfield, I was the man.

Ram used to take the piss out of me for wearing Hugo Boss suits and leaving the label on the side of the cuff. I thought that was cool, but he gave me a lot of stick for it. Ram could never be accused of being a fashion victim. He used to wear the same pair of black Tony Ford shoes all the time, which became my nickname for him. He couldn't believe that virtually every Friday I would buy a new pair of shoes. His were nice, but I think considering the dough we were on he could have afforded another pair. 'Tony Ford' got teased so much that he bought from me a pair of Jeffrey West shoes. But when he wore them we still called him 'Tony Ford'. Tony Ford played the most games of any British professional footballer, over 1,000. So we called his shoes 'Tony Fords' because Ram wore them so many times. Whether with jeans, tracksuit or dressed up, his Tony Fords always featured. If he could have put studs on those shoes he would have played in them!

Ram liked my way of geeing people up. I used to give it to someone in the dressing room if he wasn't performing. A few sharp digs to the ribs and he'd stay hit. Ram admired my fitness and dedication to training. 'When it comes to football you can never question Jamie's commitment,' he said.

One of my best mates from my Bradford days is Andrew Jackson, one of the club's most loyal supporters. He is a self-employed roofer and our friendship was forged on a lads' holiday in Magaluf,

Spain, where lots of football people go. It's best known for the alleged 'roasting' incident involving some Leicester City players a few years ago, who were accused of rape (an allegation that was never proved in court). I went with some team-mates and Jacko was with his mates. As we are roughly the same age and come from similar backgrounds on run-down council estates, we forged a bond that is still strong today. Jacko invited me to football presentations and we've had nights out in Bradford and played snooker in working men's clubs. He's followed the club for over twenty-five years and rates me in his all-time Bradford team. But he doesn't rate my dancing; reckons I'm a much better footballer than dancer and has the pictures to prove it. But what did he expect after fifteen pints?

Towards the end of the season it was between us and Ipswich for that automatic second place. That's when I played in the most drama-filled match ever. Before that game we were at home to Oxford and everyone expected us to spank them. I wasn't in the team because I hadn't played well the week before at Port Vale. We drew 0-0 and Birmingham did us a favour by beating Ipswich 2-0. The worry made me get very drunk. The next Sunday Ray, Paul Speller and a couple of other mates came to watch me at Wolves. Jewell pleaded, 'Jamie, do a job for me.' Imagine how pumped up I was.

I'm not going to forget 9 May 1999 in a hurry. The

Wolves game was frightening in its intensity, the most topsy-turvy ever. They needed to win to stay in the play-offs and went 1-0 up after fifteen minutes. We heard that Ipswich had beaten Sheffield United 4-1 so it was squeaky bum time for some of our players.

Beags twisted up Keith Curle and slotted in for the equaliser. Blakey put Lee Mills through for our second. Then Blakey scored a wonder goal after twisting up Curle again. We thought it was all over at 3-1, but that's when the drama really started. Paul Simpson scored for Wolves before getting a free kick just outside the box, which they didn't deserve. Simpson hit the inside of the post but it came out and was cleared. It was heart-stopping stuff. We'd won 3-2 and were in the Premiership. Big men started to cry.

It was Darren Moore's most memorable game. He remembers a challenge I made in the first two minutes that set the tone for the rest of the game. It was a match of incredible excitement and Darren reckons that game cemented the Bradford fans' love for me.

After that came the famous 'Macca' incident that they're always showing on TV when he fell off the top of his car, holding a drink that landed on his head, but still never spilt a drop. My quote in the paper the next day was: 'You're gonna find me drunk in the gutter tomorrow.' Journalists don't often get your quotes right, but this time they were spot-on. Raggedy little Bradford had joined the world's top league.

Chapter 14

ON THE REGGAE BEAT

Being the centre of attraction has never bothered me. That's probably why I've got into so many scrapes. I never back off, no matter how tight the situation. There is a fun side to me too, which is probably why after tiring of my pineapple hairstyle, I decided to start dyeing my Barnet for a laugh.

My cousin, Kim Johnson, who works in a hair salon in Balham, had always tinted my locks so dyeing was a natural progression. Incidentally, it was me who sported the original pineapple, long before Jason Lee also started attracting attention.

Summer 1999 and Bradford City Football Club and the whole of the city was buzzing in anticipation of our first time in the top division in our ninety-five-year history. Paul Jewell strengthened the squad by signing Matthew Clarke from Sheffield Wednesday.

Clarke was joined by three Leeds United players: Sharpey, Gunnar Halle and David Wetherall, who became City's record signing at £1.4 million.

Our first game was away to Middlesbrough at the Riverside Stadium. Yorkshire rivals Sheffield Wednesday would be our first opposition in the Premiership at the new-look Bradford & Bingley Stadium. I couldn't wait. We won 1-0 at Middlesbrough and drew with Wednesday 1-1. Andy Hinchcliffe, the left-back, used to put in their crosses all the time. I opened up his knee in a fair tackle. It was a hatchet job, but I never got booked. Heading up to the game I'd been out injured for five weeks and only trained for one. It was one of those games that leaves you feeling blessed. Four points from our opening two games helped settle the nerves.

Our fourth match was against Arsenal at Highbury. Back then Robbie Blake was a stocky forward who thought he was a babe magnet and enjoyed a laugh. He was running up his mouth with a lot of good-natured banter. We were staying at the Swallow Hotel in Waltham Abbey. He always likes to be the centre of attention so I decided to fix him by getting my bredren to ring him pretending to be an angry husband. 'You've been shagging my wife and I'm gonna kill you,' my bredren said. He rung on a hotel phone so Robbie knew he was in the vicinity. Robbie thought I might have something to do with it but was shitting himself nevertheless. He came to the room I was sharing with Darren Moore but before he knocked he listened from outside to see if we were laughing. Knowing that Robbie might arrive, we played it straight. He looked really nervous as if something was on his mind that he wanted to share with us. We were cracking up inside. We went to lunch. Robbie was already scared that we were playing Arsenal. After lunch I sneaked out and phoned my bredren and told him to ring Robbie again. 'Those two big black bastards ain't gonna help you,' he sneered at a disturbed Robbie. He really thought a jealous psycho was stalking him. Visibly shaken, Robbie looked a total nervous wreck. To put his mind at ease I told him the truth as we were going on the coach. The relief overshadowed his annoyance with us. He was really scared.

Thierry Henry gave me a hard time and when he was substituted I was relieved until I saw Marc Overmars replacing him. A tricky left-winger with blinding speed and his fresh legs I was facing total humiliation against the flying Dutchman. I almost asked to be substituted myself. At least I survived without too much embarrassment. They won 2-0 but it could have been much worse, the score line did us a favour.

With my newly dyed blond hair I took a lot of stick from the Bradford lads. But I expected it and loved the banter. I even got an unexpected reception from the Kop when we played at Anfield at the start of that brilliant 99–00 season. I'd always supported

Liverpool, so it was great to play at the legendary ground. We lost 3-1 but my best memory was the Kop chanting, 'One pint of Guinness, there's only one pint of Guinness.' They applauded when I laughed. At every ground I played, with my crazy hairstyles taunting from the away fans was normal. Everyone knew me. I was playing well so there were no comments from the opposition. They probably knew I'd play harder if they tried to bait me. But Paul Jewell wasn't amused. 'I'm not impressed: he thinks he's a Spice Boy,' he used to say. The bottom line was that I always delivered.

The wacky-coloured hair lasted for two-and-a-half seasons. Blonde, green, red, purple... you'd have to go to Dulux to make me up a colour that I haven't had. Bradford fans loved it. It was lucky I was playing well, otherwise they would have slaughtered me. Why did I do it? It was a mix of self-expression, wanting a bit of a laugh, natural exhibitionism. Professional sport has few real characters nowadays and I wanted to show my fun side. It actually helped boost my performances, I think, because with the extra attention you know your performance has to be quality.

Going out it was okay. Even the Leeds fans, Bradford's archrivals, were fine about my look. But one of the few players at Bradford I didn't get on with too well was Dean Windass. He made what was clearly a remark I didn't like and from there on we didn't see eye to eye. I confronted him and he backed off. We never got on after that.

Scoring goals wasn't the greatest asset of my game but I'm proud to say that I found the net in what is hailed as one of the most entertaining Premiership matches ever. It had nine goals, played at electric speed and some incredible quirks. Without an away goal in ages we went to Upton Park. We hadn't scored for 363 minutes. It was a freezing February afternoon which made the match seem to go on forever. With every away match the tension was building up. West Ham had lost only once all season – to Man United – so the odds were against us. Yet we scored first through Dean Windass before they hit two. Peter Beagrie equalised for us with a penalty just before half-time. After the break, step up yours truly. In a four-minute burst I sent the Bradford fans ecstatic with two quality goals to put us 4-2 up, with the faithful anticipating a third successive win. The first I snapped up after the keeper dropped a shot, and many thought the second was Bradford's best goal of the season. I turned sharply and curled a shot that the keeper could only touch at full stretch as it flew in.

Football can be so exciting because of the high drama and that is exactly what we gave the fans, albeit the home team's. It was total despair for ours. They hit three late goals to take the points. It was a commentator's dream, but awful for everyone connected with us. To top it all, Paolo Di Canio added to the entertainment by sitting on the halfway line. The crazy Italian had already had two penalty appeals turned down. When he was fouled again, he signalled to his manager, Harry Redknapp, to take him off. Redknapp refused, and Di Canio ended up scoring the penalty he craved, with Joe Cole and Frank Lampard getting the others. Lampard played so well that the media cranked up its call for him to replace Paul Scholes in the England team.

That level of excitement went on until the very last day of the season. Many had written off Bradford City's chances, right from when we first got promoted, claiming we would be relegated by February. But we hung on throughout the season, scraping enough draws and wins to reach the final match at home to Liverpool on 14 May, needing to win and the result at Wimbledon, who were playing at Southampton, to go our way to ensure we stayed in the Premiership. Wimbledon were level with City on points but had a better goal difference.

A twelfth-minute header from David Wetherall for a 1-0 win and a 2-0 defeat for Wimbledon made us feel like we'd won the Champions League and Premiership all in one match. Bradford had defied the odds and stayed up.

History was made again when we accepted an invitation to play in the UEFA Intertoto Cup competition in summer 2000; the first game for

Bradford in Europe, in Klaipeda, Lithuania. What a great season!

* * * * *

My consistency at Bradford finally earned me the call to play for Jamaica that summer. Reggae Boyz Frank Sinclair and Fitzroy Simpson had recommended me. The fax came to the club and in front of all the lads at training Paul Jewell announced I'd been selected. It was May 2000 and a mix of excitement and nerves filled me at the end of a long, hard first season in the Premiership.

I was going through a lot of emotions at the time because in the lead-up to the last game of the season against Liverpool when we had to win, I learnt that my step-dad, Dudley, had bowel cancer. He had always treated me so well, like his own son, which is why I called him Dad and it was sad to see him in pain, visibly scared. Paul Jewell couldn't have been more honest and understanding. He put my mind at ease and said he knew how I felt because his dad had died of a brain tumour. Jewell said he would understand if I pulled out of the Liverpool game at Valley Parade. But there was no way that I was going to miss it, so I still went out and played. It was of one my best games. Jewell said that performance was for Dad. It stopped Liverpool getting into the Champions League so there was immense satisfaction that day.

On top of all that, Captain Horace Burrell, president of the Jamaican Football Federation, was giving me grief. He initially invited me to join the Reggae Boyz, but withdrew the call-up when he found out about my prison past. It caused a huge controversy in Jamaica. All the phone-ins on TV and radio discussed it. It caused a storm. Generally, the public felt that I had done my time and should be allowed to play. It was a big, big thing.

I was totally mentally drained and going through every emotion. For five years my step-dad had been going to his doctor in Jamaica, who dismissed it, mentioning wind. Out there, every time you go to the doctor's you have to pay. The doctor probably just wanted money and wasn't really interested in Dudley's health. He was in Manchester, a rural part of Jamaica. I sent him immediately to another doctor, who sent him for a scan. They said it was cancer and very bad. I booked a flight for him to come to London and stay with Valerie. When I met him at the airport he looked bad. 'Are you alright, Dad?' I said, 'No, sah.' That alarmed me because he'd always been a strong, fit man. This time he looked scared. After tests the medics said he only had two weeks to live. What a blow!

With my step-dad so bad, combined with the mental and physical exhaustion of staying up, I wanted to get away for a few days to clear my head so I booked a three-day trip to Ayia Napa. Getting drunk was a convenient way of forgetting my troubles for a while.

To be fair to Burrell, after the controversy erupted a few days later he flew in with a reporter and apologised unreservedly. He even came to the hospital and explained the situation to Dudley. Initially, as a matter of principle Dudley didn't want me to play. It was at this time that the truth came out: Dudley was not my stepfather as I'd always thought – he was my biological dad. Carl Angel, a Jamaican reporter, had found out the truth but respected the situation enough not to report it. Mum had her reasons for not disclosing it, although Valerie had always known that it was Dudley and not Leon who was our real father, and she thought I knew. It added all the more to the sadness to see him slipping away.

Burrell now claims that there was widespread opposition because of my criminal past, but when he realised the depth of feeling of the Jamaican public and how much they accepted me, how they felt I deserved my chance, he conceded. He says now that because the FA had forgiven me he campaigned to get me in the team.

My mobile broke down in Ayia Napa and it was hard to keep in touch with Dudley's progress. My mates, Fat Sam and T-Bone, came with me. Fat Sam is my bona fide, the best bredren ever. In times of need he was always there. If it wasn't for them and Gee, I don't know what would have happened. Fat Sam and T-Bone looked after me proper. I was the youngest in my family and everyone was putting pressure on me. My phone broke down at just the right time out there – God was telling me something. The guys were a great comfort. From what the medics were telling me it was bad.

I got back on the Monday and went straight to the Mayday Hospital in Thornton Heath. But he had died an hour earlier. I thought Dad would always be there. I still miss him, six years on – loved him like cooked food.

We had a service in Brixton – there's a friend in prison on a life sentence who helped me through those days. Gee took me out every day and kept my spirits up. We went to bars, wine bars, nice restaurants; he looked after me proper. Gee's got a good heart. Valerie felt Burrell's attitude made Dudley die more quickly, although just before he passed away, he gave me his blessing to play for them. 'I would have loved to see you play for Jamaica, son,' he whispered. The last words my dying father said to Burrell were that he wanted to see me in the black, green and gold of Jamaica. Although terminally ill he was pleased that his dream was coming true. The day my Dad died my brother and sister came over from America. Gee had a wine bar in Lavender Hill: he opened it up for our family and close friends to reminisce. It was a free bar all night. Gee is generous, too. You can't put a price on friendship. At this time I needed good people around me: Gee, Sam, Reds, Titch (who has since passed away, God bless his soul), Speller and my cousin Steven. The two people around the most were Gee and Sam. If it wasn't for those two, I don't know what I would have done. I was on my knees and they helped me stand again.

Fat Sam has been round from the ends. The last eight years we've been really tight. When a brudda pulled out a gun on me at the Coliseum in August, Fat Sam was there for me. If you pull out a gun and don't kill me, do you think I'm just going to swallow that? Fat Sam doesn't drink. When we're out, he's just watching. Gee took us to a bar in south Kensington. It was boom, all these snobs were looking. The staff welcomed us. Afterwards he took us out of London on the A40.

Winston Clarke is another bona fide who helped me through those tough times. It was he who brought Burrell to the hospital to meet me and talk to my dad. That's when I first really got to know him. Nuff times Winston's stopped me from beating up people with just a few quiet and sensible words. We talk deeply about personal things and, if he feels I'm out of order, he tells me and I take a step back. If he asked me to drop everything and come over I'd run there. That's the level of respect I have for him, my new father figure.

* * * * *

We buried Dudley in a rural district of Manchester, central Jamaica, but it didn't go smoothly. Some of the mourners took liberties. Out there, some people see a funeral, especially when it's a decent send-off, as an excuse for a party. Many just came for the food and drink. Some were even playing dominoes on the porch. I run them. Paul Speller came out there, and so did my cousin Stephen. Dudley's best friend, Uncle Swaby, made the trip from London, too. Even out there I couldn't concentrate totally on giving him a decent farewell. Jamaica wanted me to play. I felt Burrell was trying to save face after the turmoil he put me through. Reluctantly, I started training with them, but suddenly thought: 'What am I doing here?' They wanted me to go to Barbados for the match the day after the funeral, but I flew home.

So it was a couple of months before my debut came. It may have been exciting, getting called up for Jamaica, but arriving at their 'training camp' was a rude awakening. Considering they're representing their country, international footballers expect a certain standard of comfort and luxury. I'd heard about the basic facilities at the Jamaican camp, but didn't believe it until I saw it. Players sleep in this scruffy dormitory with single beds pushed up close. They are sweaty with no air-conditioning. Talk about cost cutting! It's supposed to make us hungry, but when you're used to staying in proper hotels, it's horrible. The pitch wasn't too great, either.

At least the food was wicked, straight yard [authentic Jamaican]. I love fish now, and nuff chicken. I shared a three-bed room with Micah Hyde and Barry 'Beefy' Hayles, my two sparring people. We used to go to fish restaurants in Kingston. Some of them were in the ghetto districts and people advised us not to go there 'cos you could get shot, but we went about our business, same way, without being scared. Once, Frank Sinclair, Fitzroy Simpson and Deon Burton came and said, 'You lot are in our room.' We replied, 'If you're bad, move us.' Needless to say, they didn't do anything – full of mouth.

After our bad start, Burrell warmed to me and called me a 'truck' because I could motor through the opposition. 'You're gutsy, but also in a way very smooth in your execution of your task,' he said. Burrell was surprised that I didn't look very rugged, but I could mix it. 'You never give ninety per cent, always one hundred per cent, Jamie. That's why Coach Brown says if you're not on the pitch then he feels nervous.'

Burrell and Brown admired my man-marking skills, how I stuck to someone like glue. They felt I was disciplined and charismatic, and liked the fact that I had no fuss with anyone. They thought I played hard, but it was not my overriding characteristic. I was especially determined in games against Mexico, with players who were very clever at giving you the slip. Burrell said I was full of life and fun.

Burrell claims that some members of the Jamaica Football Federation were sceptical about me playing, but to give him his dues, he made the effort to find out what kind of person I really was and was pleasantly surprised when people who knew me spoke in glowing terms. He said that as a youngster I was 'somewhat misguided', but was 'a shining example' because of how I'd turned my life around: 'Jamie's made some indiscretions as a youngster, but I reason that if the English FA, who are some of the most disciplined people around [ironic considering the Faria Alam affair], could give him a second chance then why not offer him an opportunity to represent the country of his choice?'

Burrell claims he took a strong stance to get me selected after 'making an investigation and everyone giving glowing reports of how Jamie had reconfigured his life'.

George Evans is the vice president of the Jamaica Football Federation. He has a car rental and car dealership business in Montego Bay and is a straight, very honest man. Evans was not one of Burrell's favourite soldiers. He was surprised when Burrell called him from England, having already made his autocratic decision that I would not play for Jamaica due to my previous conviction.

Burrell thought he was taking the populist decision and was completely autocratic in not linking it through. He thought he would make a moral stand without the board's backing. When he realised the wave of opposition and his decision backfired, that's when he changed his mind. I can't prove it, but I felt that the FIFA chiefs Jack Warner and Sepp Blatter thought the same way.

've had my best times in football at Bradford. The fans are legendary.   © *Getty*

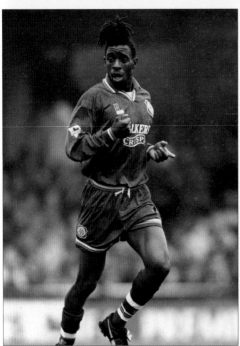

Top: Tussling with Garcia at Colchester when I was on loan at Wigan. © *Offsid*

Bottom left: My famous pineapple hairstyle during my Leicester days, 1995-6. © *Clev*

Bottom right: At one point I was dying my hair a different colour every week at Bradford. This was for our last game of the 1999-2000 season against Liverpool.

© *Action Images/MS*

A tough game between Bradford and Watford in August 1998. We lost 1-0. *© Colorsport*

Playing for Brentford during the 2004–5 season. It was good to be back in London after my travels.

© Empics

Another club, another hair colour. At Walsall in 2003. © *Action Images/Lee Mills*

Top: Midfield battle with Brazil's Zee Roberto.

© *Cleva*

Bottom: Playing for Jamaica was quality. And then there was the food…

(left) © *Cleva, (right)* © *Action Images/Alex Morton*

Playing for Bradford in 1999.

© *Cleva*

There's room for one other sport in my life, but nothing can beat the feeling of scoring the winning goal.

Evans was more understanding. His attitude was that I'd served my time and deserved a fresh start. He wasn't worried about me. Evans actually welcomed English players because he expected a higher standard of them than the locals. He liked the fact that English players can hate each other off the pitch but they are still disciplined and professional enough to play as a unit, unlike Jamaicans.

Evans even said that he found me well mannered and found my behaviour exemplary. He's got two student daughters who used to go to games and they picked Richard Langley and me out as the two nicest players in the team. Evans said that skill-wise, I wasn't in the class of Theodore Whitmore, but I brought to the game a role that completes the jigsaw. He told me, 'We like our players to be skilled, like Brazilians, but skill comes in many ways and to nutmeg a man so that the stadium stands on its feet is no less a skill than watching you terrorising a marked midfield player out the game. Those who have played the game and understand it fully appreciate what you brought to the Jamaican national team.'

Evans had heard that I liked good-looking women and said, 'Jamie is a Jamaican, after all, and if he did not gain that reputation he would not have got his passport!' He also holds me in high esteem for the way I helped my Jamaican team-mate Stephen 'Shorty' Malcolm's family after he died in a car crash in January 2001.

Evans was part of the organising team for the funeral arrangements in Montego Bay. He emailed me: 'There was much outpour of sympathy and national mourning. A trust fund was set up for Shorty's children, and even though there were many who had grown up with Shorty, played with him much longer than you, even made more money than you, none of them contributed financially in a way in which they ought to have done. Their conscience will be their guide. You're one of the few, if not the only one, who made a pledge and sent £1,000 to the fund. That, I will never forget and it says much of you. To football fans in Jamaica, if they pay to go and see skill it won't be you, maybe Theodore Whitmore, but if you are going into battle to die with your boots on, on the field, yours is the first name that comes out of the hat.'

We all hated the dormitories we slept in at training camp. There was one big dorm that held around twenty players with barely any room between the beds, so if someone broke wind, everyone smelt it. The stench worsened in the hot atmosphere with no breeze to quickly relieve your nostrils. Naturally, everyone wanted to be in the one cosy room for three. It had air-conditioning and a TV. Another time Michael Johnson and Darren Byfield rushed from the airport to reserve their beds in the little room. I turned up with Micah Hyde and Barry Hayles, and we turfed them out.

I'd known of Micah Hyde, the Burnley defender, for

years from playing against him, but only got to know him properly on international duty. We first met in Kingston at the Reggae Boyz house. I already had the No. 8 shirt and Micah wanted it too but there was no way I was going to give that up. We clicked straight away. Micah claims that the times I played against him, I tried to kick him, but he was too nimble.

The proudest day of my football life came when I lined up at the National Stadium in Kingston. It was a World Cup qualifier against Trinidad and Tobago, our biggest rivals, and the atmosphere was like a dance. It was hot too, over one hundred degrees, thirsty work. Instead of night-time, Burrell decided to make it a noon kick-off. He was trying to catch them out in the heat, but where was the logic? It was just as hot for us! Still, it was a thrill to represent my country. I loved standing there for the national anthem, even though I didn't know it. Dudley would have been proud and at least Mum was in the crowd.

I was on the bench, but after fifteen minutes, Ricardo 'Bibi' Gardner got knocked out. I went on as a wingback. The match was a blur, but I can remember that we won 1-0 and Tyrone Marshall scored just before I went on.

Jamaican football fans are definitely not like the British. They don't chant and there's no fighting between fans, so segregating is unnecessary. And they can't even begin to understand football violence. In a culture where extreme violence can be rewarded with a lot of money from criminal activity, they reason football violence is pointless if you're not getting paid.

They seem to get excited in a different way. For example, a player almost scoring from a long-range shot won't generate much excitement, but if a player does something skilful, like a nutmeg (which they call a 'salad'), they get more excited. They really respect skill more than anything, and that's why a lot of players play to the crowd. Theodore Whitmore is a prime example. Fans go to have a party irrespective of the result, victory is just a bonus. There's always a sound system blaring out during the match and if there's a goal, you often hear gun shots in appreciation from the bleachers. A lot more women go, too, looking kriss. They really dress for the occasion.

Clovis Oliveira was the coach on my debut, but he made so many poor decisions. I sweated so much, I must have done half a stone in my seventy-odd minutes. We were given lots of fluids, but that still didn't compensate. At least we won. Kingston was buzzing and we partied that night proper. It was like a British derby, but even more passionate because these are the two biggest English-speaking Caribbean sides, both with British players with something to prove. We went to the Asylum nightclub. Nuff Guinness, proper!

By now Burrell loved me up. He never knew what sort of person I was until we met, which is partly why he was so opposed to me in the first place. But Jamaica has some of its homegrown bad boys from the ghetto, who may not have done bird, but know gangsters. Burrell likes me now for being straight up and the way I play, the take-no-prisoners style. He'd say, 'Yeah man, Jamie ah bad bwoy.'

In November 2000 I dyed my hair blond when I'd first met Micah Hyde. Jamaica was playing Cuba. I never got round to dyeing it the black, green and gold of Jamaica, but it's not too late. Hyde said I was a real player's player, meaning I kept it simple and was totally reliable. He said I had no problems doing all the doggy work and admired my athleticism. Hyde wasn't bothered about 'my wrong turn' in the past and he was fascinated that I seemed to take everything to an extreme. He knows I enjoy training and feels I would do well as a fitness coach to youngsters as I can probably relate to them far better than many of my generation. I really want to pass on my experiences, good and bad, so that they won't go wrong. I'm still making the same mistakes. We all do, but someone who doesn't act on his mistakes and avoids making mistakes again is a fool. Even though we don't see each other often, Micah has a calming influence on me. We catch each other's vibe easily.

Another favourite Reggae Boy is Ricardo Fuller, the Southampton striker. The Kingston ghetto of Tivoli Gardens is where he comes from, my bona fide bredren. Ricardo came to Tiagh's christening in Battersea in June 2002. He knows I like my Guinness and thinks I get aggressive when a bit drunk. He thinks I can go any way I please. 'With your work ethic you're every manager's dream,' he tells me. 'You could even be the Jamaican coach eventually – you've definitely got that character. You always want to be involved and with discipline, you can do it.'

Club coaches and managers appreciate it when a player improves through gaining international experience, but they hate your absences and when you get injured. The game before my Jamaica debut was against West Ham and in a tackle I landed on my thumb. It was killing me, but I was so determined to play I flew out the next day. The doctor said he could pad it up and I came out with it all strapped up, but still in pain. After the game he said I should go for more x-rays because it might need an operation. I felt the doctor could have advised me better. The next day the hospital said I could have done myself some proper damage. If the doctor had told me just how bad it was, I would have had the choice. He told me it would only need a minor operation but it could have been very serious and I may have needed months out.

* * * * *

International duty has helped me bond with players I wouldn't have had the chance to. I've only known Michael Johnson of Derby for a few years, but I really like him. He was one of the Jamaicans who called me 'Cyclist' because my legs always seemed to be going in training. We used to train very early in the morning before it got too hot, from 6 to 8.30am. Breakfast and a nap, then training ran from ten until lunchtime. No matter how hard we trained, a night out in Jamaica was irresistible. I was usually the last one home and they were amazed that I would be the first one ready for training the next morning.

Johners couldn't believe that I could get back as late as three in the morning and up and ready a few hours later. In the two and three mile runs I was usually in front. Weight training was the same. He said that I was a cool guy to know but on the pitch, 'Jamie's not to be messed with'. Like so many others Johners said I was not the most technically gifted but was all heart. Off the field I was always messing around and cracking jokes but switched when it came to playing.

Johnson remembers the tackle I made in a friendly at home to Nigeria. They turned up with Kanu and some of their best players, and had the air that it would be a stroll and they'd give us a spanking. But the whole atmosphere changed when I tackled one of their midfielders early doors. We were losing 1-0, but came back to win 2-1. Everyone said that tackle changed the course of the game.

My tackles became legendary in Jamaica because they are not used to those sorts of heavy challenges. Against Haiti we were down to ten men. I was really fired up and did a fair tackle that made two Haitians somersault into the air like cartoon characters. It was the Gold Cup in Miami and they looked like they'd been in a car crash. Carl Brown, one of the coaches, said to me, 'Me nah care if you need to take two days off training, I want you to play in every game.' I was glad of that: it boosted my confidence. I thought I had to dig in, so I did, with spectacular results. The Haitians didn't come near me that day and we won.

Clovis Oliveira was the coach at the Gold Cup in Trinidad. Oliveira made me play in central midfield. He recalled Fitzroy Simpson and Daryl Powell. I have nothing against them, but resented him dropping me for them. Assistant coach Carl Brown said it was like going to war and not having your big gun. Brown knew what he was talking about because he eventually became head coach when Oliveira got sacked. Then, against Mexico at home, Oliveira dropped me again...

They were winning 1-0 and I felt Oliveira should have had the awareness to put me on. Branco was having a brilliant game and he went on to score two more. A Jamaica Football Federation official we called 'Big Mac' told Oliveira afterwards that he should have played me. He was Burrell's right-hand man and had some influence.

The next game was against Trinidad and Tobago away. Simpson and Powell were in again. At the time my partner Rowena was having difficulty with her pregnancy. We had a five-day break before the game so I rushed to England to see how she was. She was fine, but it was a nightmare to get to the game in

Trinidad. I had to go from England to Jamaica, then to the United States, to Barbados and on to Port of Spain. It took twenty-four hours to get there, and after all that Oliveira still didn't play me. I pulled him. He knew the murders I'd been through: 'How the fuck am I not in? You should have left me at home!' He gave a weak excuse about picking his best team. Of course, I wanted to go home but decided to be professional so stayed.

Trinidad had a dreadlocked player, who was taking the piss. He was killing them with it. Powell got injured so I went on and gave him one clap. He disappeared. We ended up winning 2-1 and Deon Burton scored the winner. Oliveira was a dummy, even though he was the nicest man – I prefer someone who's horrible and wins things. He got sacked soon after that. He was a good No. 2, apparently, to Rene Simoes, the coach who took Jamaica to the World Cup Finals in 1998, but Oliveira was weak. We lost to Costa Rica when we got robbed, and then to Honduras. We should have had two penalties, but when we were winning 1-0, the lights mysteriously went out for forty-five minutes. We were battering Honduras and really taking it to them. But when we restarted we had lost our rhythm and they started to bounce the ball on us. Some refereeing decisions were disgraceful, the crowd was hostile and the stewards didn't help. They won 2-1.

The next game was against The United States in

Boston in the World Cup qualifiers. If we had won
and the last two results had gone our way, we would
have scraped in. For me, that game was a mixture of
emotions. The US were 1-0 up early doors, but then I
scored one of my best goals ever. I chested the ball
down and hit it on a left foot half-volley. Chris
Kamara was commentating for Sky Sports and said, 'I
didn't know he had a left foot.'

Later on, the ball came over the top and I'm looking
at it, but Aaron 'Spider' Lawrence has gone for it and
landed on me, breaking my left arm in the process.
The physio came on and at first thought it was a head
wound. Imagine my frustration when he's trying to
treat my head when I'm in unbelievable pain with a
broken arm. The adrenaline allowed me to play on,
but when I made a tackle it was too painful and so I
had to go off. As I was rushed to hospital, the
Americans beat us 2-1 from a penalty. They wanted to
keep me there, but it was a few weeks after 9/11 and
that day the Americans were going into Afghanistan.
That's why the atmosphere made me nervous and I
insisted on going home.

British Airways upgraded my flight with Fitzroy
Simpson and I drank about five bottles of champagne
to try to ease the pain and make me sleep. The arm
wasn't in a cast, but a bandage and splints, and the
bones rubbed against each other. It was the worst pain
I've ever had. I had to have a metal plate put in. At the
same time a niggling groin injury was repaired. With

one arm and not being able to walk, I felt disabled. Anyone with a grudge could have given me a volley then. They were rough times, but my prison days were rougher – an injury mends faster than a prison sentence.

Representing Jamaica made me a better player because it was at a higher level against world class guys. I began to pass better and Bradford players like Wayne Jacobs noticed. That's when Bradford put me in central midfield.

English football is all rough and tumble, one hundred miles an hour. Playing in the Prem, you obviously have to have ability, but at international level you need more range. I found myself reading the game better, getting more patient, I saw the passes earlier and generally felt more like I was the man.

I played in two rounds of World Cup qualifiers in 2001 and I was voted the Best Jamaican Player in 2002 by a Jamaica supporters' club in America. They came all the way to Bradford to present me with their award after a match. It was a proper presentation in the sponsors' lounge. Brilliant!

My last game for Jamaica was against the United States in the World Cup qualifiers in Boston. It was freezing. We needed to win to go through, but drew 1-1. That was on 11 November 2004. Coach Brown did his best but we weren't quite good enough. That's when they decided to blood the next wave of Reggae Boyz. It was the end of my international career. Coach Brown was sad to see me go. He loves me like cooked food. Coach Brown can take some credit for me wanting to inspire kids because he once took a group of players to a youth club in Boys' Town, a Kingston ghetto where Bob Marley grew up. The others gave speeches and then Coach Brown invited me to speak last. I'm not one for speeches but I broke it down to them in patois, not to pick up the gun but to do something positive with their lives. They gave me a big cheer 'cos I had more in my locker than the others.

That was the end of my international career. President Crenston Boxhill sent all the dropped players a thank you letter stating that Jamaica was going to concentrate on younger, homegrown players. But I had no animosity: I was thirty-four, started my international career at thirty, and enjoyed the whole experience of playing in forty internationals, including friendly matches. If necessary, I would have played for Jamaica for nothing: it was a thrill, plus I got to see my mum as well. We had bare jokes when socialising. I loved every minute of it: the fans, the sun, cheap Guinness. Paying only $100 Jamaican (£1) for my favourite tipple was lovely. I tried the locally brewed Dragon Stout – nice, but it can't compare with the genuine black stuff. The other popular drink out there is Wray and Nephew white rum. The great reggae singer Delroy Wilson used to drink it for breakfast. No wonder he died of cirrhosis of the liver at forty-seven! It's about a million-proof, a mad man's drink, Devil's juice... Give me a pint of the black nectar any day.

Chapter 15

CRISIS VALLEY

Dad had just died and I was still grieving. They were sad times. After the jubilation of beating Liverpool on the last day of the 1999–00 season to keep us up, it all went downhill from there. Paul Jewell rocked us by walking out on Bradford to join Sheffield Wednesday. It came as a shock to many, considering he had kept us in the Prem against all odds, but everyone has his price and they must have made him a great offer. It turned out that Wednesday got him there under expectations that were too ambitious. The grass is not always greener!

At Bradford, Jewell was able to work without the weight of expectation. That was certainly not the case at Wednesday which had been one of the founder members of the Premier League and recently relegated from the Premiership. While the club's supporters expected success and an immediate return to the Premiership – a demand further boosted by their decision to sell season tickets under the guise of a 'Premiership Return' marketing scheme – behind the scenes it was chaotic. Many thought they overspent on Wim Jonk and Gilles de Bilde, while others on big money, including Simon Donnelly, Andy Hinchcliffe and Phil O'Donnell, were frequently injured. Players were sold or given free transfers, but with many highly-paid players unfit they could not be removed from the wage bill. That further held Jewell back and a lack of support from the board failed to help matters. Eventually he left due to poor results, but his situation was impossible because there was no money for him to buy the players he really wanted and needed.

Jewell and I had an unwritten agreement that he would take me to any club he managed. He tried to buy me at Wednesday, but Bradford wanted £1 million – liberties considering they had only paid £50,000 for me. But now I was a much better player and if they were going to sell to a Yorkshire rival, they weren't going to give me away. Had Bradford dropped the asking price to maybe £600,000, a deal might have been made because they knew how much I wanted to get away. More than any other manager, Jewell made me play for him. I'd go an extra mile, run through brick walls, the lot for him. Only Martin O'Neill came close out of all the other managers to make me feel fully appreciated.

The only funny moment I recall from them times was when Rodney Marsh, the Sky pundit, came to our first home match in September 2000 and had all his long hair cut off on the pitch. The previous season he used to coat us off [criticise unnecessarily] all the time. He'd been running up his mouth saying we weren't good enough to stay up and, of course, we proved him wrong. That was his forfeit. Fair play to him, he took it well, made him look better, actually.

Miserable, I returned for the start of the next season deliberately late. The new manager was Chris Hutchings, Jewell's former No.2. But my mind wasn't right after the trauma of losing Dad. Although I played in the Intertoto Cup, the usual enthusiasm just wasn't there. They took me all the way to Russia even though they knew I had a bad back and no chance of playing, all that horrible way to leave me in the stands. Boy, was I cussing. The Intertoto Cup is one of those pretty worthless ones and hardly registers as something to be proud of winning, yet we were in it. As it was our first time in European competition and there was no telling when we'd next get some, it must have been a case of take it when you can. It must have been solely for the money. Then it was to Holland for a game against RKC Waalwijk. We won 1-0, but I was still upset. Two weeks later we beat the Zenit St Petersburg 3-0 at home. Having got that distraction out of the way, the next assignment was not a problem to get motivated for.

The first game of the Premiership was away to Liverpool. Anfield beckoned: the stadium I'd always dreamed of playing at. Imagine how I felt when Chris Hutchings took me all the way there – and left me in the stands again. After the game I went to see Emile Heskey in the players' lounge, but I thought the team coach deliberately left me there with no money. Heskey's my tight bredren. He came back to give me some dough and I got a lift home. I phoned Hutchings and told him to get me out of the club or I'd swing for him. Obviously scared, he claimed he didn't receive his phone calls because there was no reception and that's why it was going straight to voicemail. I asked for a transfer because they weren't paying me what I was worth and I had only asked for a little increase in my wages.

Considering I had helped that team avoid relegation from Division One and been one of the key players taking them into the Premiership and kept them there against all expectations, it was not an unreasonable request. Especially as it was not very much anyway compared to some of the other players. At the time the wage structure was total madness. They were bringing in players on huge salaries (like Benito Carbone, who was getting £40,000 a week). Some of the others were on big dough, too. I asked them for only £2,000 a week more and they weren't having it.

To show you how off-key the set-up was, that summer they'd smashed the club's transfer record by bringing in David Hopkin from Leeds for £2.5 million. He may have been a former Scotland international midfielder, but to put him on the kind of dough he was on – about £25,000 a week – was madness. I was earning a fraction of that.

I never played in the first six league games, which yielded only one win: 2-0 at home to Chelsea. When they played me, that's when they started their best spell even though some of the results were going against us. At least we were more competitive. My first league game was the 1-0 loss at home to Southampton.

Two days later I faced my old team-mates at Doncaster in the League Cup. With the poor form we were showing in the Prem, some predicted an upset. But we made sure that didn't happen, winning 7-2. It remains our biggest win in the competition.

West Ham away was our next game. I had to mark a teenage sensation, causing a buzz in midfield, who everyone tipped to be an England regular. Even at eighteen he was extremely accomplished, brave, skilful with a good spirit, always coming back for more. That day Joe Cole made an impression on me and I'm not surprised that he's such a big star now.

* * * * *

To help forget my troubles, partying was as strong as ever. Luton, my cell-mate from Dover days, kept in touch and around that time I was getting a lot of grief from these local bad boys, from Chapeltown. I was seeing one of their girls, and they resented it. They were jealous of my status as a footballer and the tension was building up. All my bredrens – Titch, Scotty, Luton and a couple of others – came up on the Friday tooled up 'cos these guys had been threatening me. I'd recently been burgled and suspected the local boys were responsible. My mates came with shooters, a stun gun, samurai sword, the works... We were going to have it out with the Leeds mob. Luton came in carrying his weapon in a big heavy bag. We thought it was something that could really do some damage – maybe an AK-47 or bazooka. He pulled out a massive... bicycle chain! We fell about. It was so unexpected, we could not stop laughing. Luton tried to style it out by saying it was an industrial chain with vicious spikes on each cog, but it still looked like a bicycle chain. How he was going to use that in a tear-up, I don't know.

As nothing happened that Friday night we were more relaxed and decided to go to a nightclub in Leeds – Nato's. Michael Duberry, defender at Leeds United at the time, was in there, and he started trouble with the local lads by coming on to my girl, stirring things up. The locals got vexed. They started crowding round me because Duberry had wound them up. I was ready for it to kick off but Luton pleaded with me to leave and tried to push me out. 'You can't be fighting in a nightclub, blood,' he said.

'You don't want to lose your job. Besides, we need you in there to get us tickets.'

Andy Myers was with us and to his credit he stayed and was ready to have it. Unlike Duberry, who showed that when the going got rough he hit the road. Everybody wanted me out of the club to avoid trouble, but I wanted to have it with them so sneaked into the toilets. A few of them came in looking for us. Luton, Scotty and me smashed them up. Long after Duberry left, Luton persuaded me to get in a cab. There was a scuffle but the bouncers quelled it. That night, because none of my friends had got lucky I took them to a brothel: Winston's. Luton played pool. He didn't indulge, but the others certainly had a good time.

When given a chance, that season I was playing the best football of my career. Injury-free, motivated and settled in my personal life, I was totally committed to seeing Bradford stay up. The crowd appreciated it, as did my team-mates, but the club still gave me no more money. But I wasn't drifting in and out of games anymore and taking on people for fun...

Stan Collymore joined us on his travels in October 2000. He scored on his debut: a 1-1 draw at home to Leeds. People say he is this and that, but I got on alright with him. He was on £20,000 a week and I felt he deserved his dough, even though he only lasted five games. Man like him and Dean Saunders you can't knock them because when it's in-the-trenches stuff they're there. Benito Carbone befriended me. His wife and kids lived in Italy and visited him in Leeds occasionally, so when they were away he was lonely and relied on me heavily. To relieve the boredom and for that edge in sharpness strikers are always looking for, I took him for extra shooting practice after training and weight-training round his house. Carbone turned out to be extremely lazy and showed his true colours when he eventually left; he didn't even bother to phone to thank me and say goodbye. In my view, he was the biggest waste of money the club ever spent and he helped make it bankrupt. In fifty-four matches for Bradford matches he only scored four times. No one was sorry to see him go.

When the chips were down some players disappeared, but I was digging deep. Hutchings was sacked after the Charlton game away, which we lost 2-0 that November. I played wicked. Perhaps Hutchings was out of his depth as he only lasted five months. Stuart McCall and Neville Southall took over for a couple of games. At least they picked me because they knew that when it came to digging deep in a relegation battle they could count on Jamie Lawrence. Macca didn't want the job so they appointed Jim Jefferies who lasted for just over a year until December 2001. A big Scotsman, who'd done well at Hearts, but there were question marks over his ability at this level. Sensible new managers give the squad they inherit every chance to prove themselves, but he never fancied me. He wanted to bring in his own players too quickly. Jefferies must have spoken to Fitzroy Simpson about my past. What were my chances after that?

Ask any self-respecting footballer whether he loves what he does and it doesn't matter if he's a semi-pro posting letters in the week to supplement his football earnings, or a multi-millionaire Brazilian World Cup winner, he will say, hand on heart, that playing is a bigger buzz than the money. That was always my attitude, whether it was for Camp Hill Prison or Bradford City against Man United. That's why it was so frustrating under Jim Jefferies, who did not believe in me enough to put me in consistently. It was the odd game here, sub there, dropped there, and it was doing my head in.

Because Jefferies wouldn't play me, I asked if I could go. Jewell was at Wigan by the end of that season but he wanted to take over my contract and wanted me to move closer to the club. I didn't want to move house, so decided to stay and sit out the two years of my contract, if necessary. Soon after Jefferies arrived, we played Spurs at home when Ledley King scored the fastest goal in Premiership history after ten seconds. We still had eighty-nine minutes to score and sure enough, we scraped a 3-3 draw with me scoring one of them. It was a scrappy one, from a corner, after someone flicked it on and it ricocheted off me. But, hey, they all count. We lost 3-0 at Chelsea next and I played really well. For once the manager and the coach, Billy Brown, praised me. On that basis you'd think I'd be guaranteed a place but logic didn't play a big part, it seemed to me, in Jim Jefferies' way of thinking. We lost heavily at home to Sunderland on Boxing Day and then I didn't get a look in until the return match against my old club a month later. We got a goalless draw at Sunderland with me having a good game at wingback. Then Jefferies dropped me again and I got recalled a month later when the club was already effectively down, against West Ham at home. We lost 2-1 and to compound my frustration I went up for a header, landed badly on my thumb and was out of the side for two more months whilst I had an operation on it.

Jamaica needed me and, when the thumb was almost healed, I went on international duty. I'd literally stepped off the plane on my return when Jefferies picked me for Everton away. Andy Myers scored in our 2-1 loss: a bullet header, the only one he's ever scored judging by how many times he talks about it.

Andy's a great lad, speaks his mind when he has to and I respect that. The first time we really clicked was on holiday in Ayia Napa, on Nissi Beach. It was a boiling hot day. Everybody was in flip flops, or bare-footed. I was wearing my shoes. My feet are not the prettiest and I was very self-conscious that day. Andy took the piss. He reckoned crocodiles have got better feet. 'You could use your feet for ashtrays,' he said.

To show how poor our form was, we took a third-minute lead but missed two penalties against Everton. Liverpool, my dream fixture, at home was next. On a scale of one to ten, my excitement level was twenty. That week there was a big buzz in training. Pitting my wits against the likes of Steven Gerrard, Gary McAllister and Michael Owen was one to savour. All my bredrens came up from London to make a weekend of it, including 'Tyson', a mate from way back. I couldn't have been happier. Until I was dropped and then I was gutted. What a let down! They won 2-0. Owen scored one. For me, it was a big disappointment. Jefferies was bang out of order; he knew how much that match meant to me. Sometimes managers like to play God just because they can; it's an ego thing. But for the good of the team it can be totally detrimental. No wonder players lose patience and rebel.

At least I got to play Middlesbrough, who had Dean Windass in the team. It was a great chance to vent some of that anger and worth the booking to give him a good kick. I had a blinder that day, set up our goal beautifully. I jumped up, went on an amazing run, toe-poked it to Wayne Jacobs, who knocked it in. That goal gave me as much satisfaction as scoring it myself. We drew 1-1.

Already relegated and going through the motions to save professional pride, we went to Leeds for the final match of the season, 13 May. This fixture is always edgy 'cos the rivalry is so intense. We were never in the game and it was 4-1 well before half-time. Everyone in the side seemed to be arguing and it came as no surprise when Stuart McCall criticised Andy Myers, who told him to fuck off. It kicked off. Andy chinned Macca and that right-hander split his eye. Benito Carbone didn't like Macca, so when Andy punched him he was pleased. 'Andy Myers, you are my hero,' he said. Everybody was arguing. We were falling apart. We hadn't been functioning right as a team all season and this was the final straw. It was the weirdest, craziest thing. Coming against Leeds made it ten times worse. I hate losing at the best of times and this was one of my lowest points.

In the changing room at half-time our keeper, Aiden Davidson, was kicking bottles all over the place in fury. For Aiden to be losing his rag like that was very unusual. Ian Nolan had a stand-up argument with Jim Jefferies, who felt he was to blame for the fourth goal. Harry Kewell had gone round the defence and Jefferies blamed Nolan. Nolan is normally the sweetest, easy-going guy in the world, but he just lost it. 'You cunt, you've ruined my career!' he shouted at Jefferies. We couldn't believe it. At the time Nolan travelled with Dean Saunders a lot and he sounded just like him. We reckoned that Dean had coached Nolan to have a go at Jefferies because it was completely out of character. Dean must have told him, 'Don't have it next time Jefferies has a go.' Talk about funny. We ended up losing 6-1 to our sworn enemies in our last game in the Prem after a horrible, horrible season: my dad had died, I'd broken my thumb... I'd also had a groin operation and broke my arm that season, plus we got relegated... Could things possibly get any worse?

Chapter 16

SURVIVAL INSTINCTS

For a professional footballer the close season is supposed to be a restful one, but in the summer of 2001 I was criss-crossing the Caribbean playing for the Reggae Boyz. We faced the USA at home in the CONCACAF (Confederation of North, Central American and Caribbean Football Association) World Cup qualifiers and victory was vital. In the cauldron-like heat of Jamaica's National Stadium we played them in the burning afternoon sun. Everyone was melting, and we hoped the Americans would be, too. I had a shot cleared off the line. Claudio Rayna, the tricky midfielder, had to deal with me that day but he didn't get much of a look in. The heat got to the Americans, plus we played a high-pattern game. We had so many chances but our finishing was poor and that came back to haunt us as we drew 0-0. Still, it was a good point.

Four days later Costa Rica away was a big challenge. The stadium had the most hostile atmosphere I've ever experienced. I could sense how the crowd hated us. When we went out, they were booing for fun. The atmosphere was really felt. Paulo Wanchope, another England-based player, was brilliant for them; Onandi Lowe scored a world-class goal for us. I had a penalty turned down. We had chances galore in the second half when we were on top and looking set to win, running them ragged. They didn't know how to handle us.

Suddenly the lights went off so we had to go off – it lasted half an hour.

They came back fresh and we'd lost our rhythm. What made matters worse, was the ref: he gave everything their way and us nothing. It was like playing twelve men. We couldn't even get a free kick. It seemed if you even breathed on them, they acted as if they'd been shot. After, we made an official complaint but it was thrown out by FIFA. Wanchope scored one and they got another to win 2-1. Daylight robbery!

Anyone who plays at Mexico's Azteca Stadium starts at such a massive disadvantage that they should give all the away teams a two-goal head start, it is that hard. We played them in the Gold Cup. The stadium is thousands of feet above sea level. When you play at altitude, ideally, you should allow six weeks there to get accustomed to the thin air. It literally takes your breath away just to do anything physical. In the Gold Cup things got worse. The Mexican officials claimed there had been too much rain on our training ground so we couldn't train. Was there nowhere else suitable in the whole of the city? In the end we had to train in the hotel grounds around the flowers.

In those conditions, imagine what it's like to play a high-tempo match for ninety minutes – mission impossible; it was scary. As soon as you get off the plane you struggle to breathe. Azteca Stadium is heavy; it's enormous, the biggest stadium I've ever played in. Imagine filling a ground with 115,000 hostile fans. Behind cages. That's nearly twice the size of Old Trafford, which holds 67,000. The intimidation worked. I felt like a little pin – I've always prided myself on my fitness but after doing one run it felt like ten.

Their left-back knocked the ball forward and scored in the first two minutes. That's when we all knew it would be a long game. They killed us; we just couldn't run. It was obvious why they hadn't lost at home for a number of years. We got slapped 5-0. Unfair? It's their country! If Jamaica could dominate at home like that I would love it. But we wouldn't put the opposition at an unfair disadvantage – it's not in our spirit.

That night we went out to a lap dance club. Certain man had a dance. When the bill came it was $1,500, about ten times what it should be. They tried to skank us and things started getting ugly. It looked like it would kick off. One other big man came over and told the bouncers we were paying $800 tops, take it or leave it. We came to an arrangement and paid it, even though we knew we had been ripped off. In Jamaica we treat everyone alright. Only Honduras comes close to the sort of intimidation we got at the Azteca.

They're all behind cages and their fans deserve it. They were swinging non-stop like monkeys.

* * * * *

That summer I went to Hatton Garden and before going on holiday to Jamaica I bought a ring, a nice subtle little thing with a diamond. Rowena and I travelled by Air Jamaica business class. We stayed at the Grand Lido Hotel, one of the loveliest places on the north coast of the island. Aaron 'Spider' Lawrence, the Jamaican keeper, lived nearby and provided us with a driver. I took Rowena to some waterfalls. What a lovely, relaxing atmosphere. The next day I pulled Spider aside and told him I needed a boat to take us out in the moonlight because I had something to tell Rowena. His bredren had a nice boat and about ten of us set out in it with nuff food and drink. Everyone but Rowena knew what I was planning. I was so embarrassed, but felt compelled to do it for the woman I love deeply.

So did I go down on one knee? She was lucky to

get the proposal – I had a reputation to maintain! As I took her aside, people knew what was going on. It was very romantic. Rowena was very emotional and I thought she was going to bawl. She phoned her mum in Ireland to tell her and she swears that night she conceived. The proposal must have started her ovulating! Little Tiagh was born exactly nine months later on 25 April 2002, Rowena's birthday, so I've no excuses to forget such a significant day. We were going to get married in Ireland soon after, but when Rowena became pregnant we put it off and still haven't got round to it because of circumstances. Moving clubs in the past couple of years has meant living like a gypsy. At least Rowena can boast that her engagement has lasted longer than all my others put together.

Her family are quality. Her parents are Mary and Mick Whelan – nice people. Her brothers, Mick and Warren, and sister Sally are just like Rowena: warm and giving, with no airs and graces; no hint of racism either. They just check people for what they are. They always make me feel welcome when I visit them in Carrick-ma-cross in the Republic of Ireland. We go to a pub called Jonjo's. I once took money off the landlord after betting him one hundred Euros that Arsenal would beat Man United for the Premiership. Mick reminded me of the bet. Top man!

* * * * *

In the pre-season, Uriah Rennie, the controversial referee was in charge. We were playing Rotherham. I was warming up and pinged the ball, shanked it and hit him on the back of the head. It was purely accidental, comical as well, but dignity crushed, the pussy threatened to book me. Idiot!

The next season I thought everyone would get a chance at Bradford. I'd played well enough to convince Jim Jefferies I was worth a shot, but he started with his own boys. When I did play we tended to do well, winning six, drawing one and only losing once in my eight games, even though I was not fully fit and injured for some of the time. At the end of October Jamaica played USA away in another World Cup qualifier. Things looked promising and I scored. Chris Kamara, commentating for Sky, raved about it. Not only did we lose 2-1, but I broke my arm and came back needing a groin operation, too.

Bradford tried to get me fit, but by the time I was ready at Christmas, Jefferies was sacked. For me, not getting a fair crack throughout his time eased the disappointment of seeing him go. It didn't help Jefferies that he didn't get on with the captain Stuart McCall; they'd had a massive bust-up.

Someone had to go and it weren't going to be Macca. Jefferies could never win that tussle. By then the chairman Geoffrey Richmond was picking the teams. Ridiculous? Yes, but Richmond was no ordinary chairman. Jefferies resented it, and

Richmond had backed him into a corner, so decided to sack him. Richmond seemed to like me, even though I was asking him for more dough.

All the expensive new signings like David Hopkin and Dan Petrescu had gone and Benito '40 Grand' Carbone was loaned out. Not being a Premiership club anymore they couldn't afford those wages. I felt I was worth a couple of grand more a week than they were paying. After all, I'd helped take them into the Prem and kept them there. But no, they refused. I felt Geoffrey Richmond was wrong but he's not the sort of person to admit it, even though, in my view, he was bang out of order spending so recklessly on players who didn't fit in.

Nicky Law was brought in at the beginning of 2001 and I knew I needed to win him over. He never knew much about me. 'Who's this geezer?' I could see him thinking. But after he saw the way I trained and played, I was first one on the team-sheet. But the club paying huge sums to a few players had depleted it financially and we were broke.

Before he arrived Nicky Law had heard a lot about me, not all of it good. He admitted my reputation had preceded me, but he was pleasantly surprised and we hit it off immediately. Nicky loved my commitment and desire to win, and would say, 'If I had eleven Jamie Lawrences in my side, the team would pick itself every week.' He liked my toughness, but appreciated my personable side, too – and he saw how

I was encouraging and nurturing the youngsters. As a black guy coming from the streets, who has not totally gone down the bad route, Nicky felt I had a lot of experience and knowledge I could pass on to wayward youngsters, too, and being a mentor really appealed to me.

Nicky was impressed with my fitness and felt I was a better player than I was given credit for. Because of my versatility, he played me in several positions: 'You're not just a hustler and bustler, Jamie, you can actually play, too.' I never gave him any trouble and I think I won his respect, which is why, when he moved on to Grimsby in March 2004, he gave me a chance there.

New Year, new manager… Injury-free, I was ready for battle and came back at Barnsley on 19 January 2002. They were winning 3-1 and taking the piss before Ashley Ward and Lee Sharpe hit two late goals. I set the tone as soon as I came on as sub; did a tackle and licked up someone. Yep, that did the trick!

Two weeks later Grimsby away was my first full game, a vital game. Both teams were in relegation trouble. I played centre-midfield and had a blinder. My passes were accurate and I was winning tackles. It felt great to be back. Most matches are won in midfield and I had a blinder. We lost at Wolves before going to Gillingham on 12 April 2002.

The day before Gillingham I'd attended my friend Titch's funeral (he had been killed in a tragic accident). Nicky Law was very understanding and gave me time off. Titch had been at a party and some nutter in the next room shot someone. The bullet passed through the victim, through the partition wall and into Titch's head. What a terrible way to go! He was only thirty. A big Liverpool fan, I got a Nicholas Anelka Liverpool shirt signed by all the team for him, which was placed above his coffin. He had a proper send-off with six white horse-drawn carriages and thirty white doves were released. Brixton came to a standstill that day.

Determined to do well at Gillingham, I lobbed a 35-yard shot over the keeper, sweet. It was so out of the blue there was stunned silence at first. Everyone joked that I didn't mean it: a fluke, I'd tried to cross it. But it was one hundred per cent intentional and dedicated to Titch – a great goal for a diamond geezer (that wonder strike was actually Bradford's Goal of the Season). We beat Gillingham 4-0, so it was a mixture of emotions.

Scoring was never my speciality, but I surprised myself by finding the net in the next game, at home to Nottingham Forest. With two minutes to go, Lee Sharpe crossed it. I climbed above the centre-half and powered it in for the winner. That was a nice 2-1 victory, which helped relieve our relegation fears. I've scored a few with my head – I like to attack the ball.

Maybe the satisfaction of winning two on the bounce lulled us into a false sense of security. We lost the next four, then drew twice before beating Crewe and getting a draw at Watford. The final game was at home to Norwich on April Fool's Day. It was a nothing game for us (we were already safe from relegation), but they needed to win to ensure a play-off place. I had a shot kicked off the line. Then my volley was heading for the top right-hand corner: a screamer. I turned to celebrate, but somehow someone got a foot to it – I still don't know how – and turned it away. They won 1-0. It was a disappointing ending in fifteenth place. We'd hoped to go up.

I'd had a good season, but having just come out of administration, the club was still on its knees with no money to buy. Looking at the quality of players we had in the side, like Macca, Ashley Ward and Sharpey, we were underachieving. It wasn't Nicky Law's fault. We had to get out of this rut otherwise things could get worse. We'd done our job by staying up, but there was still a lot of turmoil at the club.

At least I had another Jamaica game against Nigeria to play two weeks later at QPR in West London. The rivalry was as intense as ever. Playing just down the road from Harlesden, where so many Jamaicans live, gave us the extra incentive. But it didn't work and we lost 1-0.

Chapter 17

END OF AN ERA

The whole squad had been sacked. Considering only a short time earlier we'd been in the Premiership generating millions from sponsorship, gate receipts and TV money, the situation was ridiculous: no wages for weeks. Fifteen of us refused to play in a friendly at Hull City. To make matters worse, Carbone was rumoured to have got an £800,000 pay-off to return to Italy. He was so ungrateful he disputed paying the tax, insisting the club should pay it. Imagine how we felt!

For four months from April 2002 we didn't get paid. The club tried to go into administration. I was in Ayia Napa and Sky Sports News reported that nineteen players had been sacked. Within ten minutes I got a call from Colin Lee at Walsall, another from Sheffield United's Neil Warnock, and then there was a third. When I came home there was a lot of confusion and rumours flying around. The Professional Footballers' Association (PFA) came down hard on the club to reinstate us. Poorer players were struggling. The PFA gave us £5,000 each, which helped but it was not enough. When all the players went back for pre-season training, I refused. But after a week Wayne Jacobs said I should come in. We still hadn't been paid and nothing was sorted out. I had to take a percentage cut. They were hard times when everyone thought we were candidates for relegation, but I wasn't having that.

To make matters worse, my house in Leeds was burgled again. They stole my passport, preventing me from playing for Jamaica in America. The Jamaica Football Federation tried to sort out an emergency one, but the passport authorities refused to co-operate, partly I suspect because I'd been burgled so much and had so many passports stolen, they probably thought I was running a racket. It was really frustrating because I definitely would have played, but that was typical of my bad luck at the time.

It was a traumatic time, but I just got on with it. My attitude was that actually playing helped take away the stress. Not many people would be prepared to go to work for four months, knowing they were not going to get paid. 'You have to ignore what's going on behind the scenes and coming to work helps you to forget about it,' I told the media. 'We're also doing it for ourselves because if people come to watch the game and you're available on a free transfer, then they are going to be impressed with you.'

In June 2002 I got a decent offer to join Sheffield United. It was tempting. My daughter Tiagh had just been born and I'd recently bought a house in South London. It may sound crazy, but despite the crisis, my loyalty still lay with Bradford. In August 2002 I'd just started getting paid again and genuinely enjoyed being with my team-mates. To me, sticking out an extra year until my contract ran out seemed the best option. We had to tighten our belts and so I cancelled our holiday that summer.

Despite the desperate times, I was still confident we would be strong enough to challenge for promotion back to the Premiership. Only Ipswich seemed outstanding that year.

Bradford chairman Geoffrey Richmond was a notoriously tough negotiator, but he wasn't all bad. When Chris Kamara signed me, he admitted having reservations because of my criminal past. He made a point of meeting me and spent three quarters of an hour chatting. 'You know, Jamie,' he said later, 'I found you so open and honest in everything you said. There was no attempt to hide your past, or cover your time in prison. You weren't proud about what happened, but you would talk very candidly about it.' Richmond joked that I was the toughest player at the club and if I ever came in and asked for an increase in my contract, he would never argue. 'How much do you want? Is that all! Fine by me,' he joked – I wish that was true.

Richmond's favourite memory of me was when, as part of a pre-season tour one year, the players were sent to Chester Army Barracks for a week. 'The lads were absolutely horrified at the standard of accommodation, the food and the tough regime,' Richmond says. 'Jamie was in his element – "Listen lads, I've stayed in a lot worse places than this. And for a lot longer!"'

Richmond started to take out millions in dividends from the club when he realised he'd overspent and put most of the money in his wife's name so he couldn't be made liable for the debts. He declared himself bankrupt and thought he'd got away with it. It was poetic justice then that they broke up, she took all the dough and left him broke.

There were a lot of misconceptions about my criminal past. Talk about Chinese whispers! Anyone would think I was a serial killer. Jim Jefferies believed I was a murderer and many of the Bradford fans reckoned that, being a Londoner, I must have been a hit-man for a drugs baron. On a Bradford City website someone wrote: 'Jamie's £50,000 transfer fee didn't match the amount stolen in various armed raids!'

* * * * *

But at Stoke two weeks into the season there was another crisis. As someone tackled me, I went to turn and my studs stuck in the ground. I tried to go on, but the pain was too much. Luckily, it was a non-weight-bearing bone, the tibula of the left leg, which was broken. I was only out for six weeks. Although not fully fit, I made my return at Reading. They sent me for intensive physiotherapy at Lilleshall and it did wonders. The physios worked on my injury and fitness all day, every day, for three weeks. By then I was nearly ready. At Lilleshall the regime is proper: you treat every day like you're going to work, not as if you're a patient. It lasts from nine till four and if your injury means you can't sit, you have to do everything standing up. After all that, you play volleyball at 4.30 and there are forfeits if you lose, such as 2,000 metres on the rowing machine or a million chin-ups on the gymnastic rings. Worse day to lose was Fridays because the loser had to ride a push-bike two miles to the campus gates and back. If you cheated and got sussed, they'd drop you in the middle of Stafford and make you ride miles back. We called Fridays the Champions League Game. The winners would be driving away and waving to the poor bastards left behind!

The favourite pub for anyone staying at Lilleshall is the Barley Mow. It's in Newport, a few miles away, and well worth the trip – modern, a good size, with friendly staff who wear an all-black uniform. It's even got a dance-floor at the top end with a resident DJ and opens till 1am at weekends. Regulars tend to sup their pints and watch the footballers and sports people from Lilleshall knock back bottles of Dom Perignon. That was exactly what a bunch of us were doing one night when the bouncers got a little jealous. I'd just ordered an £80 bottle of Dom when one mouthy bouncer told us to drink up rapid. Last orders had just been called, so we thought he was being a little bit hasty. We felt that they shouldn't have served us at all, if that's how fast we had to down it. Scott Eustace, who was playing non-league at Hinkley United, took exception to the big lairy one and shouted at him to fuck off. He came over and Scott shoved him. The bouncer dropped as if he'd been shot and we fell about. Embarrassed, the bouncer and some of his goons wanted to have it out with us. Me, Scott, Billy Mercer, Tony Crane and a couple of others were ready to go to war. But it didn't kick off as the bouncers knew their man was out of order and also, we were good customers. We thought that was the end of it...

The next afternoon as we were working out in the gym, Steve, a physio, came in, looking very worried, and said there was a Range Rover with tinted-out windows outside and four big men were looking for me. 'Uh-oh,' I thought. 'Here we go again.' The rest of the man dem didn't want any of it. I've never seen so many people shitting themselves, but being me I decided to front it. The men looked menacing. One man stepped forward. I was ready to have a go, despite the odds:

'Jamie Lawrence?'

'Yeah.'

'You were in the Barley Mow last night, weren't you?'

'Yeah.'

He held out his hand. It was the Barley Mow's owner (I think his name was Paul). He wanted to apologise about the previous night and admitted the bouncer had been out of order. That night we ended up having a bottle of Dom there on the house and even started raving with him and his mates.

One day in a practice match I played centre-half, even though I didn't feel right. I must have played well because Law and everyone else said I was like the brilliant Italian defender Franco Barese. On the Friday we arrived for a Millwall game and I was surprised to be in the team. Although we lost, I played well – Law loved me that day.

Dave Wetherall was one of the few big signings at Bradford who proved to be worth every penny of the £1.4 million they paid for him in 1999. A big defender, he missed most of that season with a groin injury. His career was thought to be over at one point when he kept breaking down – he only played six games from April 2002 to March 2003 – but he's a good pro and was always one for the bunkers.

The club physio, Steve Redman, liked my cousin Adrian, who came to train with us for a trial. But he was not fit (I actually wanted to get him away from the bad influences in London and thought a trial at Bradford would give him time to clear his head). Nicky Law didn't want my cousin, but he was a little nervous about telling me. Later, Law told me he felt lucky to be sacked because it meant he didn't have to tell me Adrian wasn't good enough! Bryan Robson took over and brought his own players in.

* * * * *

To help forget my troubles, partying was as strong as ever and I was still in touch with Luton, my cell-mate from Dover days. I love Luton: he's so protective. He felt I was always roughing up the manager, if not in the team. In the early days, if I was dropped, I would text them over and over again. Luton would always tell me to hold it down and just be patient. Although we don't see each other often and I move around a lot, Luton always tracks me down by finding out which club I'm at and phoning them. He pretends he's a close relative – which he is in a way – and they get in touch with me. Luton's most cherished time with me was not in prison or partying, but the night he came up to Leeds and we went to a bar and just chatted and reminisced over a couple of drinks. I was desperate to get back to London them times but he talked me out of it.

Luton cherishes the Emile Heskey Liverpool shirt with all the team's signatures on it. He has it framed beside his bed. It's a green away one and was very special to me because it was from the game when Bradford had to beat Liverpool on the last day of the season to stay in the Premiership. I was going to keep it, but Luton persuaded me to hand it over – he's never washed it.

It was a great bunch at that time. Aiden Davidson, the mad keeper, kept things interesting with his crazy antics involving bodily fluids. He says I tried doubly hard to score past him in training and never did – in your dreams, Aiden! A bit of a card sharp, we had plenty of games of Hearts on the team coach. 'We let you win occasionally to stop you from losing your temper, Jamie,' he said.

Another character was the Liverpudlian Eddie Youds, who joined in 1997. He came from Leicester with Nicky Morvan and Gavin Ward. Youds thinks the fans liked me because I played with my heart on my sleeve and was prepared to run through brick walls. He rated me as the biggest team player at Bradford, prepared to do anything to make the team better. Eddie respected Bradford for giving me a chance and felt it made me a stronger, better person. He was really pleased for me when my Jamaica call-up came in 2000. If I was hyper before, I was even more full of life then.

In Jamaica I was well respected. I got my head down

and the coaches loved me for my work ethic. They took me off the wings and liked to play me in more central midfield. The Jamaican supporters' website reggaeboyz.com even voted me Best Player in our World Cup qualifiers ahead of higher-profile players like Theodore Whitmore, Ricardo Gardner and Deon Burton. Even though we didn't reach the World Cup Finals, they appreciated me for overcoming adversity in the early days and more than proving that I deserved to be in the side. Initially, I thought it was a wind up, but when it turned out to be genuine, I was ecstatic. They even asked if I would be happy to receive the award at Bradford. They sent the award from Florida, where they are based. I was the first person showered, dressed and in the players' bar on the day I received it.

Another proud moment I can take to my grave. One Reggae Boyz fan who really appreciated me is Sam Green, a shipping trader based in Kingston, who comes to England on business regularly. He stays in Lavender Hill and drinks in the Beaufoy Arms so we've become great friends. 'I hope your book changes the lives of young people who were going astray and improves their attitude,' Sam told me. 'It should help any youngster to move in the right direction and use their talent and creativity in a positive way. The first time I met you, Jamie, was in the Beaufoy. You showed your humility by giving your uncle the money to pay for a round of drinks rather than big-up yourself by flashing your cash. I respect that. I was one of the fans that gave you a thunderous applause on your debut and wish you were still in the side. The way I see it, even if you're fifty, but playing well, you're still good enough to get picked. Roger Milla went on forever for Cameroon and you deserve that chance too.'

* * * * *

Of the admin staff at Bradford, I have a fondness for Anita Smith, who was personal assistant to the chairman. She covered up for me during my occasional absences and protected me a lot when it came to dealing with my tangled love life in the early days and little indiscretions. Anita would say, 'Tasha's just phoned and she says she wants her money before you go to Harvey Nichols!' I adored my kids and provided for them, but Tasha wanting £800 a month for baby Nathan was a bit steep.

The time I missed the trip to St Kitts because of injury and went off to Ayia Napa Anita was an angel. Paul Jewell would phone regularly and ask if I'd been getting physio treatment. Even though Anita hadn't seen me, she said she'd spoken to me (which was true) and I was fine. What Jewell didn't realise was that she didn't have a clue where I was. Anita reckons I used her like my personal PA: 'Jamie, you're more demanding than the rest of the players put together, but at least you're the nicest!'

Anita liked the fact that I didn't give it the Billy Big-

Time. Some players had their heads up their arses when it came to relating to the fans, reserves, support staff and apprentices, but I wasn't like that. Nothing was too much trouble: shirt signings, autographs, charity work: it was no problem. Fans were helping pay my wages and it was the least I could do. When I first got called up for Jamaica Anita was a darling. She knew how anxious I was to get it, and sneakily told me before Jewell had the chance to in front of the lads, and so I had to feign surprise.

She has another memory of me that I'd completely forgotten about: when Lee Sharpe joined us. There was a little resentment because Sharpey had played for two of our bitterest rivals – starting at Man United before moving to Leeds. He was also on £13,000 a week, a lot more than many of us who had been at the club a long time. Anita was with a group of us including Ashley Westwood and Sharpey in a club in Harrogate. As we were walking into the club, some thugs in the queue started abusing Sharpey. Two of them got really lairy in the club and were spoiling for a fight. It was going to kick off. I stepped in, had a quiet but firm word with them and quelled it. Anita says she breathed a sigh of relief.

* * * * *

Footballers always make headlines when there is a nasty incident in a nightclub. Even the most unknown player with a tiny Division Two side can get unwelcome publicity if there's an incident and most of the time it's not their fault. It's usually some little prick trying to impress his drunken mates, or wanting to earn a few quid by selling the story to the papers. That's exactly what happened to me one February night in Leeds in 2003. A bunch of pussy-holes in the club thought they would have a go, but not being brave enough, one of them blindsided me and whacked me with a knuckle duster. The cowards didn't only outnumber me, they didn't even have the guts to take me on one on one. They broke my cheekbone in three places. There were fears that I would be out for two months, but I've always healed quickly and was back in action within a couple of weeks, though wearing a protective mask. It was a vicious attack. The club was concerned that the eye socket was damaged. At one point they considered fining me two weeks' wages, but when I explained what had happened they were more understanding.

Even wearing that mask, I had one of my finest games at Coventry. Nicky Law told me to mark Gary McAllister as best as I could. The wily Scot was nearly forty, but still slippery enough to dictate games, if given the time and space. Looking like a stand-in for the *Phantom of the Opera* may have been odd, but I was so fired up it didn't matter. McAllister only evaded me once, so I clattered him and got booked for it. It was well worth it against someone of his class.

We won 2-0 – very satisfying. 'What I did out there was what I do all the time for Jamaica,' I told the eager reporters. 'Stopping the playmaker is a job I have done before. It might not be the most enjoyable thing, but I will do whatever it takes to win, and it worked here. He is a very talented player, but I had a job to do and I did it.'

At Bradford I hit it off straight away with Gordon 'Flash' Watson when he joined, partly because he was a Londoner, too. Flash claims we were like brothers at one point: we attended Lilleshall at the same time with injuries and had a lot in common. Two weeks after joining Bradford he broke a leg. We were in the same hotel, having joined at the same time, and have sons who are roughly the same age. I gave his son Callum one of my Jamaica international vests and he was really excited. We also played pool a lot. Flash is another one who couldn't believe my energy levels. 'You burn the candle at three ends,' he joked. Although we were good mates, Flash felt I led by example to stupid extremes when it came to drinking and partying, as if I had something to prove. I don't think so: it's just how I am.

Flash reckoned I had no finesse, but he changed his mind the day I ran down the right against Reading in January 1998, cut in and bent the ball into the left corner for a superb goal. 'I thought you was just a battering ram, Jamie. You surprised me there,' he said.

Watson is a very sociable person, but as brave as they come in a tight situation. One night in a Leeds nightclub some racist pricks picked a fight with me. I was out with Flash and another player, Mark Prudow. The idiots surrounded me and although I was ready to battle my way out, Flash jumped in, pulled me away and confronted them. With no thought for his own safety, he defused a situation that could have got very ugly.

Often a joker, when Flash heard I had a stud in my dick, he wondered if I was exploring the wrong avenues. Then, when I dyed my hair blond, he thought it was all that Guinness rising to the top. He was amazed at the number of mobiles I had, too. I'm down to two now, but in those days Flash reckoned I had more phones than Jack Nicklaus had clubs! He wasn't always a joker, though. Flash was the first high-profile player to successfully sue another player for causing him a career-ending injury. He won a seven-figure sum in damages and now puts his personality to good use selling property in Spain and Portugal. These days, with the sort of money players enjoy, they no longer have to get low-paid, menial jobs when they retire from the game and Flash is a perfect example.

Although Flash didn't stay long at Bradford, we had such a strong rapport that we're still in touch years later.

You meet lots of different characters in professional football; it's what makes the sport so interesting. Until the nineties players were usually from white, working class, British backgrounds, but not anymore. The game is so diverse now. At Bradford I saw them all in every race, creed, colour, shape and intellect. Footballers have an unfair reputation of being dim, but someone who lived up to that image was another midfielder who I shall call Innocent. A nice kid, but thick: fast feet, but his brain weren't too sharp. He got into the wrong company at his first club, in Merseyside, and even when he joined us, he was still being bullied. They were trying to extort £10,000 out of him and he was scared, so I spoke to them. 'He ain't giving you Jack,' I told them. They backed off. Chances are, if you give an inch they're going to take liberties.

Bradford City fans are top drawer, faultless. I'm a footballer most fans would love because I give one hundred per cent every game. Fans love that and usually chanted my name. My favourite end at Valley Parade was the McDonald's Stand. Usually I was on the wing and two-twos we'd normally be kicking at the away fans end in the first half. The second half we'd be playing into the McDonald's Stand and the fans used to urge me on. That's when I knew they loved me: I was one of them, from the streets. They identified with me. Many fans play football, but few make it and I just happened to do so. They made me feel more appreciated. I only had a few low times at Bradford, even when the managers got in players to replace me, they always reverted back to me.

For me, the love of the fans was very important, which is why I kept in touch with Jacko and Timothy 'Bobsy' Hague, who was paralysed three years ago in an accident when he was up a ladder at work. Only twenty-three, he's a life-long Bradford fan. He broke his neck and damaged his spinal cord, and is in a wheelchair but gradually improving. His brother Charles is a photographer at Bradford and said that I was Bobsy's favourite player, being a battler. Having the commitment to run the length of the pitch to make a tackle was what he liked to see me do. He was in the Pindersfields Hospital, Wakefield for eight months and I went to see him with Andy Myers. Wayne Jacobs visited a few times, too. Even though I'm down in London we've kept in touch. Bobsy saw me playing for Walsall against Bradford and I arranged to meet him after the match. I gave him a Jamaica shirt, which he's framed and put on his wall. His face lit up when he saw it.

* * * * *

Leaving Bradford was sad. If the club hadn't gone into administration I like to think I would still be there today. I didn't want to leave: it has a great family atmosphere. My contract ended on good terms and I received glowing recommendations in the local press. I give credit to the club, they couldn't stand in my way and despite offering me a new contract, I decided to move on.

FROM PRISON TO THE PREMIERSHIP

I joined Walsall on deadline day, 12 April 2003. Without having a chance to play in the Gold Cup, I had to fly back from international duty in Jamaica. It was total madness, because in my haste, I left my car keys in Jamaica. I had to get the tube to meet Silky in Potter's Bar. He drove me the one hundred miles there and we arrived with only ten minutes to spare, just before midnight. I still had my Jamaican tracksuit on.

Respect for a fellow player is not a word I use lightly, but I have plenty for Stuart McCall, my old captain at Bradford. He was a Scottish international, started his career at Bradford City, played at the highest level for Everton and Glasgow Rangers before returning to Bradford soon after I joined. A fiery ginger midfielder, he calls himself a strawberry blond.

We got to know each other really well through snooker matches. I beat him easily, but he always told everyone he was the better player. Macca set a high standard on the pitch that inspired us. He would spray the ball out to either Peter Beagrie on the left, or me on the right. Macca realised that he'd get wizardry and skill out of Beags, and from me aggression, speed and power. As my career went on and I moved more into central midfield Macca helped me get the best out of my game. We'd do skill drills the day before a match with maybe three teams racing to wind in and out of five cones. Everyone would do their best to dribble around them, but I'd smash my way through.

Macca would take the piss. 'It doesn't matter what you do on a Friday, Macca,' I'd say, 'it's what you do on a Saturday that counts.'

Macca was no shrinking violet in a tackle but he told me he'd rather play with me than against me. If a move broke down he was grateful I'd be the first one getting back. 'Full backs are always guaranteed a hard time with you, Jamie,' he'd say. 'You're not the most skilful crosser, nor fastest, but on a cold, wet Tuesday night when nobody really fancies it, you're right in there.' He felt I was a great part of Bradford's success. Macca wrote his autobiography years ago, in which he included playing with the likes of Paul Gascoigne and Peter Reid.

Always a joker, Macca said, 'You liked the girls, Jamie, but they didn't like you.' At least I think he's joking!

Macca reckoned I played my best in London, in front of my mates. 'Your game goes up ten per cent in London, Jamie. Look at the facts: you don't score many, but got two goals against West Ham and one at Spurs when we drew 1-1. You seem to need to feed off that energy.' He had a point. That Spurs game was on my birthday, March 8 and I was determined to score to celebrate my 30 years. I had a limo waiting after and Miss X gave me a blow job back to the hotel. We freshened up and changed, then we partied in the West End at Sugar Reef and raved downstairs until 2am when we went to the Coliseum. Ended up with Miss X again and another blow job on the way to Chelsea Village, where I fucked the life out of her. What a day!

Macca is now assistant manager at Sheffield United and he was one of the reasons why I felt so confident we would do well that season. But my optimism for that 2002–3 season was misplaced. So many quality players moved on and, with all the uncertainty and troubles, it was unrealistic to expect anything better than survival in that division. At least Bradford finished nineteenth, six points above Sheffield Wednesday, who were relegated.

My final Bradford game against Wednesday has bitter memories. I got sent off for two bookable offences, but I blame Danny Maddix. After a foul, he wound the ref up, but the ref decided I should go – that was low.

I'd already left when Bradford's season finished: it was the right time to move on.

Chapter 18

SAMBA LESSON

My football career has been truly blessed. Imagine coming into the game at twenty-three with no previous experience at professional level and within a few years to be playing in the Premiership, winning a League Cup medal and playing at international level. The icing on the cake definitely came in facing world champions Brazil in a friendly at the Leicester ground. Jamaican kids grow up aspiring to be as good as the Ronaldos and Rivaldos of this world; no other heroes compare, never in their wildest dreams do they expect to play against them. I was lucky enough to live that dream. The match was confirmed a couple of weeks before. Praying not to become injured or ill in the days leading up to it, I felt like a kid waiting for Santa. I had been injured at Walsall when I came back from World Cup duty in the summer. Colin Lee promised he was going to give me extra time off – I never wanted to play, anyway and needed a break.

Going to Jamaica to play for them was quality, especially when it was freezing cold here. Their facilities were appalling compared to English standards but the camaraderie and team spirit were exceptional. It also gave me a chance to link up with friends and family. Going away for a week wasn't too bad but any longer and I desperately missed Rowena and the kids. Missing a lot of Tiagh's early baby years was tough. Every time I came back from a trip she was doing something new.

Walsall's form was terrible. We'd lost all the previous seven games and my relationship with Colin Lee was non-existent. It was hardly great preparation to get into a winning mindset, but at least I had no injury worries after starting the season late with a broken toe. I was buzzing, especially as it was clear when Brazil arrived that it wasn't a substitute team. All the big names were there except Ronaldinho. I travelled to Leicester with Deon Burton. There was a great sense of déjà vu when we got to the Hilton Country Club, the same place where I'd signed eight years earlier for Leicester. The memories came flooding back. How far I'd come in that time, little old me playing against the mighty Brazil – bet the Camp Hill screws wished they'd taken bets on that happening. All them times I was in jail training my bollocks off, not knowing where my life was heading, this was something I never thought could happen.

Aaron 'Spider' Lawrence was my roomie. I really checked for him because he was one of the first Jamaican players who welcomed me after all the controversy over my past. Some of the players made me feel unwelcome when I joined the Reggae Boyz and I had wanted to leave straight away. Spider was cool. I would go out with him and a journalist, Carl, and eat fish – bare respect for both.

That Friday night I was bursting for the game to come and every second seemed like an eternity. Playing the game over in my mind again and again, I just wanted to be sure I did myself justice. Deep sleep was impossible. On the Saturday we trained at Leicester's training ground. It was the same place as before, only they'd improved it by laying better pitches, expanding the weights room and cafeteria. I made sure I got the match programme, which is still a treasured item. Many of the lads had already faced Brazil in the Gold Cup a few months earlier, but it didn't dent their excitement. Who wouldn't be excited? It don't get better than that!

After training there were a lot of tickets to sort out. We'd only got two comps each. My bredrens came to check me: I had to buy at least fifteen and we only got twenty-five per cent of the gate but that's business. Jamaica is not rich like England. Brazil may have been the bigger draw, but we packed it up. Under Coach

Carl Brown we had a small practice game. He always, always picked me, never any doubt. Ojay, Emile Heskey's best friend, took me to the barbers. A trim on the eve of a match was my way of taking my mind off things and giving myself a psychological boost. Then we went shopping for CDs just to waste some time. But the nagging feeling of worry about my performance would not go away. I always set myself high standards and this was the ultimate test. The kid in me kept saying, 'God, please don't make me embarrass myself.'

Jamaica travel with their own cook, which guarantees chicken with every meal: jerk, curried, stewed, grilled, steamed... You name it, he can do it, as long as it's chicken. By now, pasta (for the carbohydrates) was my choice the day before a big match. It helps with stamina and energy levels – Yard food is too heavy. Chicken is alright the day before, but I prefer pasta. On the day of the match I sometimes had fish.

That Saturday night I watched TV without concentrating. I was listless, agitated; tried to sleep early, but couldn't and ended up flicking through the channels just to while away the time. I managed to get six or seven hours, but it wasn't heavy, deep sleep. Spider wasn't the first-choice keeper, so he knew he probably wouldn't get on, which is why he was calmer. How was I going to do tomorrow? Please God, no humiliation. The Walsall players, including

Paul Merson, predicted we'd get lean up – four or five nil. I was thinking, 'No, we're not gonna lose; certainly not gonna get beat up.'

One of the legacies of doing bird is that you tend to wake up very early – there's no choice in jail. Waking my roomie was something I tried to avoid. I showered quickly and went for a full English. I tried to chill, but my mobile was blowing up. Everyone wanted tickets, even Walsall players I hadn't expected to come were phoning, including Junior, the Brazilian forward. I got him one. Andy Impey, who was at Leicester then, came for two tickets. Everyone wanted to know me that day. Only the Bradford-Liverpool game when we needed to win to stay in the Prem rivalled that day for ticket demand – and this was only a friendly! Eventually I became irate when people wanted to chat.

The others had lunch whilst I stayed in my room. Then the coach came to take us to the ground. Every stage of the route to the stadium was a roadblock; it took forever. People who don't usually go to football were there: old West Indians, black women, black families, ex-pat Brazilians... It was an amazing carnival atmosphere. Jamaicans and Brazilians are the biggest party people, so it was expected. Whistles, horns, drums, bandanas, flags, klaxons, there was noise and colour everywhere you looked. They're poor, but they know how to have a good time.

The ground was packed. Little Leicester couldn't match the demand that day, even though the Walker's

Stadium holds 32,500. Thousands were left outside waiting in the futile hope of getting in. Our coach was pretty silent, everyone deep in their own thoughts. Yard dancehall music was playing. I left a couple of tickets at the box office with Claire, who remembered me from years earlier, and gave me a big kiss and cuddle.

In the dressing room we went over our shape again: it would be 4-5-1. I was central midfield. As I was changing, the same thoughts came, 'Don't make a fool of yourself.'

It was a bright autumn day. I went out to warm up, then did the team warm-up. The ground was heaving. Rickan, my friend Winston Clarke's little boy, was our mascot, but I can't remember much about looking after him because I was so focused on the game. I didn't even hear the crowd.

Vicky Vixen, aka 'The Fox', Leicester's mascot was geeing up the crowd – sexy blonde. We'd had a fling in my playing days there: done the business, nice memory…

Coach Brown gave us our final instructions. Ricardo Fuller would be up front on his own. Deon Burton had to stay wide right and we all had to keep it tight and maybe catch them on the break: simple. Lining up for the national anthems I wished that Dad was there, but I knew he was watching. Mum was in Jamaica.

Brazil's players are on a different planet: they're like Martians, they're that good. They played well within themselves, apart from Rivaldo, who was trying to impress 'cos he was looking for another club. The rest were just enjoying the workout. The first thing you notice about every Brazilian is that he is comfortable on the ball, like he was born with it at his feet, and it's never left him. Everything they did was second nature. They're all athletes and blessed with incredible strength – that's a quality completely ignored by most observers, how strong Brazilians are. It's not just their skill and technique: they are all supermen, really hard to knock off the ball – wicked class.

Every significant fact about that day is imprinted in my mind. It was on 12 October 2003. Their team was Dida, Cafu, Lucia, Roque Jnr, Roberto Carlos, Gilberto Silva, Emerson, Ze Roberto, Kaka, Rivaldo and Ronaldo. Adriano was just coming through – he was one of four substitutes. I rate them all, except the centre-back, Roque Jnr: he didn't impress. Our team was Ricketts, Ziadie, Davis, Sinclair, Gardner, Whitmore, Langley, me, Marshall, Fuller and Burton. After seventy-two minutes I came off, totally exhausted. I'd done better than expected 'cos I thought I'd be substituted at half-time.

The game was a blur, just a magical feeling, the whole experience. I was a defensive midfielder that day and really played on instinct and adrenaline. It's usually easy to pick up a threat, but they were rotating positions so much you didn't know who to stay with. Brazil are like the Harlem Globetrotters of football: you expect their dominance to end like the West Indies in cricket, but it never has – they always find that extra level. Rivaldo is a great player, but I've seen better left-footed players, who didn't get the accolades. That day Ronaldo was on fire, full of tricks. He sent Frank Sinclair for a pie and I'm sure he's still wandering around the ground. Ronaldo made out he was going to shoot and he sent Frank down, but didn't shoot. In the same move he shot, but the keeper saved it. Brilliant!

Roberto Carlos scored a worldy goal in the fourteenth minute. We thought it was going to miss, but he swerved it so much that it crept in – Deon Burton was dragged off because of it. Instead of trying to flick the ball on, he tried to chest it down but lost it. Roberto Carlos seized it and buried it with that vicious swerve, similar to the one he scored in France with a worldy free-kick. For the rest of the match Brazil played well within themselves: exhibition stuff.

From that game I learnt I had a long way to go from being at the proper top. England always bang on that they have world-class players; if so, Brazil are universe-class – they come from space. Jamaicans have traditionally styled themselves on the Brazilian way, which is why we keep getting their coaches. The most successful one was Rene Simoes, who took them to their first and only World Cup Finals in France in 1998.

Brazil's moves were second to none, far superior to England's. I can't see past Brazil winning the next

World Cup. They just keep churning out this remarkable talent – the list is endless...

Two days later I played for Walsall at Watford. There was a tiny difference in the atmosphere – what a comeback to reality. Coach Brown came to see me, which was nice. Walsall was unhappy that I wasn't at my best, but hey, it's not every day you get a chance to play Martians.

Chapter 19

RIGHT SIDE OF
THE LAW

L eaving Bradford was tough and it was with a heavy
heart that I joined Walsall with the intention of
staying for two years if they avoided relegation from
Division One. I told the Bradford fans I'd had so many
great times there with so many good memories; it was
like leaving my family. 'I know the fans are gutted to
see me go and the gaffer rang to wish me well,' I told
the *Telegraph & Argus* newspaper. 'I think I've been
more appreciated in the last two years than in the
previous four. The fans have always been good to me.
They know what my game is all about and I think
they enjoy a good tackle as much as a great pass.'

The last time I played at Valley Parade was in a
charity match in May 2004. It was a very emotional
day for me because I hadn't had the chance to say

goodbye to the fans and players properly a year earlier. I got a proper standing ovation and it was all I could do to hold back the tears.

'I was meant to be in a training camp with Jamaica, but I couldn't miss this,' I told the local press. 'I've spent more of my career at Bradford than anywhere, and they will always be close to my heart. The last couple of years there weren't the best as the club was in deep financial trouble, but I want to show my appreciation and do anything I can now to help.' To this day I believe that if the club hadn't struggled financially I would probably still be there, helping them in League One, or maybe they might never have gone down. It still pains me to see Bradford hit hard times, especially considering that not so long ago they were in the Prem. With the right finances I'm sure they can bounce back.

Walsall were six points off the bottom three when I first joined. The manager Colin Lee wanted a bit of battling spirit so that's why he signed me. He claimed he wanted, 'some fire and aggression'. Although it was a wrench to leave Bradford, it was nice to have a bit of security, so I thought. At the age of thirty-three, players in the lower leagues are generally getting a little anxious about their future, especially towards the end of the season.

Lee knew me from when I was at Leicester and he was first-team coach. We were staying in the same hotel and he used to look out for me. He'd been chasing me for a year and had been on my case when we all got temporarily sacked the previous summer. With that kind of enthusiasm I expected to be an automatic choice, anyone would. Anyway, I'd had such a tough time meeting that signing deadline that I would have thought any manager would have wanted to adopt me as a long-lost son.

This is what I went through to get to Walsall in time. I'd left on the Monday to link up with my Jamaican team-mates in Kingston for Gold Cup games against St Lucia, Haiti and Martinique. When I flew out, it was to Cuba first and then on to Jamaica, which took twelve hours. I trained on the Tuesday, preparing for the St Lucia game the next day, but got a phone call to come back to sign for Walsall. On the way out my bag was left in Cuba and that only arrived in Jamaica a couple of hours before I had to come back. Three pairs of Nike trainers had been nicked from the bag. When I got back to London I realised I'd left my car keys in the house in Jamaica. So I took the tube to Cockfosters, which is thirty-six stops to meet Silky, who drove me up to Walsall. It was a nightmare! I still had to pick up a spare car key from Leeds and travel to Heathrow to fetch my car.

It all started well. My debut came at Gillingham, where we won 1-0. At first Colin Lee played me regularly and we got enough points in the final matches to stay up. I went off for international duty that summer looking forward to the season ahead. My form in the Jamaica matches was good. We had two low-key friendly matches, then beat Paraguay at home 2-0 in another friendly. I had a good game. Before the match, assistant coach Peter Cargill (who later died in a car crash) paid me a top compliment. 'When we go to America, we really need you, Jamie,' he said. It boosted my confidence no end.

Against Columbia in the CONCACAF Gold Cup we were roasting in the one hundred-degree heat. We had our chances to draw, but lost 1-0. We then played Guatemala in the Gold Cup. That day Onandi Lowe was skipper and really hyped up. Before the game Guatemala were trying to wind us up in the tunnel with all this abuse in Spanish. Lowe was shouting at them, 'Talk fucking English!' He scored a world-class goal, but was too hyped up and got sent off just before half-time. It was exhausting with ten men, but we won 2-0.

I knew I was tired, fatigued, when I got back to England. I'd had no break, but I was no idiot. I'd just played five games in tropical heat and had only six days off throughout, that was the level of my dedication to the Reggae Boyz. During that time I'd gone from Jamaica to America to Mexico and then back to Jamaica before coming home.

International duty had made me too jaded to start the 2003–4 season with Walsall and Colin Lee had promised me a long rest. But he had a crisis and asked me to play forty-five minutes of a match before I was really ready. As luck would have it, near the end of the half, one of my own strikers went up for a header and landed on my toe. It was very, very painful. At first the physios didn't think it was serious, even though I was in a lot of pain. It wasn't until a black American physio, Dr Rogers, spotted the real injury that it was attended to. It was a broken toe so I was out for six weeks.

At Walsall our training games were always very competitive. Paul Merson ('Mers') had just arrived and because of his Arsenal-England background, everyone treated him with a lot of respect. But I'm not really a respecter of reputations and I tackle everyone the same. A challenge on Mers was a particularly hard one and the whole game stopped. It was one of those moments when everyone cringes and holds their breath to see what happens next. Mers swore at me but I looked at him hard and nothing came of it. Afterwards Oz said, 'Trouble with you, Jamie, you see the ball and not the player. When you go to win it, you don't know how to do it half-heartedly.'

One day after training Mers got out of his pram. He thought he could take liberties and started taunting me in front of our team-mates, claiming he could outbox me if we ever got in the ring; he reckoned he could jab my face off. I said, 'I'm getting vexed! If you don't shut up, Mers, I'll fucking knock you out and put you in the boot of my car!' He picked up his phone and walked out, and he never challenged me again.

After a couple of weeks, Colin Lee phoned: 'Do you

fancy playing forty-five minutes on Saturday because we lost last Saturday?' But I wasn't ready.

Walsall started the season well. They beat West Brom 4-1 in the opener and Mers scored two wonderful goals. We were unbeaten in our first four, then started dropping points.

I returned in mid-September, but my first four matches were losses. In those first few games I hadn't regained my full fitness and that's when Colin Lee started playing around with me. He seemed to lose faith in me, even though I was playing as hard as ever, never shirked a challenge, ran for lost causes, tackled like a demon... the usual stuff that had endeared me to him in the first place.

One of my best mates at Walsall was Simon Osbourne (we had the same agent in Silky). I met him in a Greek restaurant in Waltham Abbey, near Silky's house. We had previously played against each other when Oz was with Gillingham. We had a ding-dong, very competitive. Walsall won 1-0 and Oz remembers kicking me so hard he damaged his foot. When Oz arrived at Walsall there were a couple of faces he already knew, including me. I had a bit of a fearsome reputation and everyone was amazed when Oz took the piss out of me straight away.

Jimmy Walker was our keeper. At the time of writing he is in the Prem with West Ham. I called him 'Donnie Brasco' after the Johnny Depp character in the film of the same name, starring Al Pacino. He's only five foot eleven and weighs over thirteen stone; the wrong shape for a keeper, but Fat Boy always gets the crosses and never gets chipped. Jimmy reckons I tried to clatter him when I played against him, but he was too quick – I don't think so. When I arrived at Walsall he knew one of my nicknames as 'Shabba' because of my hairstyle and my 'Loverman' reputation. My prison record went before me and some of my new team-mates were a bit wary, but Jimmy just took the piss from the off.

We enjoyed some classic nights out at our special restaurant, the Bombay Spice Indian, in Birmingham. The owner would close it down for us to eat, drink and be merry – wild parties till the morning, lots of laughs.

Every summer Jimmy joins a bunch of us on a lads' holiday to Marbella. On the first one we went to a club with mirrors all round. Totally drunk, I decided to leave before the others and waved them goodbye. Ten minutes later I still hadn't left and walked back to them. The lads said they thought I'd gone. Got talking to someone, I claimed, and said goodbye again. But it happened again: I returned a few minutes later and made another weak excuse. This time they followed me. With all those mirrors, it was impossible to find the exit. In my drunken state I had to feel my way around for the way out. They creased up watching me and when my face lit up when I'd found the exit it was all they could do not to reveal their amusement. The next day Jimmy asked if I'd got out the club okay. Before I could answer, they fell about again. Being lads on holiday, we ate out all the time despite being in a luxury apartment. On the morning of our third day we wanted to air the room and thought a curtain in the corner hid a window. Pulled back, the curtain revealed a pristine kitchen – the cleaner must have thought we were the cleanest, tidiest footballers in the world!

Nicky Thomas is a close friend with a wicked sense of humour. On holiday in Marbella last year we had these drinking games using playing cards. The highest card had to drink a shot. I dominated on the first day, ruined them. To get me back when I was losing on the second day (I got so drunk), they switched my drink to sun tan lotion. I thought it was Bailey's! I passed out, but the next day I felt worse and got the shakes – I had to stay in for the whole day feeling like shit but it didn't ruin my holiday. Freaks come out at night, that's me. Sometimes I can be flagging at nine, ten, whatever, but come midnight I just pick up, and that's when I could drink for Jamaica and England combined.

* * * * *

Don Goodman, who I first bumped into as a player at Sunderland back in 1993, was by now a player-fitness coach at Walsall. So determined was I to sustain my playing career, I went for sessions with Don after regular club training. He pushed me to my limits – endorphins must have been popping out of my head. Always impressed with my strength and general fitness at Sunderland, by now Don was amused at how people bounced off me. We even did kick boxing together to reach that extra level of fitness. How Colin Lee wouldn't play me in that shape, I don't know.

The turning point in my relationship with Lee came at Sunderland. I ran my bollocks off that day, but we finished with ten men and lost 1-0. No disgrace, but Lee decided I was the scapegoat. After the match, his daughter's boyfriend, Aaron Kerr (reserve keeper at the time) texted me to ask if I was going out that night. But it seemed obvious it was the gaffer who really wanted to know. I texted back and said I didn't know. I stayed in anyway because I didn't feel like it, but it wasn't out of fear of Lee. What I naively didn't realise was that Kerr was informing on me about my partying.

The following Tuesday, 21 October 2003, we were away to Reading. After the Sunderland performance I was on the bench, which was a bit ridiculous considering how I'd run my heart out. I only went on for the last nine minutes. We lost 1-0. Colin Lee's conscience must have been killing him. When Aaron Kerr broke up with Lee's daughter I kindly allowed him to stay in my house in Wolverhampton for two weeks, rent-free. Some people have different morals. Colin Lee needed me. We were in a war in the relegation zone. He thinks he's a brainy guy, but I'm one step ahead of him... Aaron Kerr was coming out with us and informing Lee on us.

After the way Colin Lee pursued me, we should have had a fantastic rapport, but our relationship quickly disintegrated. I had a big problem with him and he felt the same about me. He says we always got on fine and he admired my enthusiasm, but that didn't match the way he treated me. Lee had a problem, not with my attitude as a player, but with my social life. So why go out of his way to sign me if he had a problem with my off-field behaviour? It just didn't make sense.

Towards the end Lee played every player available, except me, in a desperate bid to avoid relegation and getting the sack. He must have known I would do a good job. Lee claimed he wanted me back, but he didn't play me. Politics...

Martin O'Connor – good pro, honest as the day is long – was the captain when I arrived at Walsall in April 2003. We roomed together for my first away game, but he left before me for apparently the same reasons: Colin Lee promised him something, but it didn't materialise. When Lee promises you something you have to check how many knives are in your back. Walsall wanted to pay me to go, but offered foolish money. I told my agent, who was by then Tony Finnegan.

I didn't seek any advice from Silky. Until then I was on good terms with him, but I'd heard things. I'd like to knock him out now! Years later I found out from a very reliable source that he done a wrong 'un on me which I'll never forgive him for. I was on holiday in

Marbella and bumped into him in a bar. He came over to shake my hand, but I wasn't interested. When I asked him about it, he denied it, but by the next day he kept ringing my mobile.

When, after the twentieth time, I finally answered it, Silky invited me to compete for Jamaica in a free-kick competition against David Beckham, Roberto Carlos and all these big names. He was only trying to butter me up through his guilt. The things I've done for that man, no wonder some agents have a bad rep! He's threatened to sue me if I put these allegations in. Well, here it is Barry Silkman, I'm calling your bluff – I had a good relationship with you and not just professional!

When Silky's disabled daughter died, aged five, I helped him a lot during his time of grief. I went round to his house and drank a whole bottle of Wray & Nephew white overproof rum with him to help drown his sorrows. It hurts me that someone I checked for did that. I thought he was different from most agents.

Generally agents are only out for themselves. If they get you the best deal possible you've got a result, but many get paid by both club and player, so there's often a huge conflict of interest. Sometimes an agent can be good for a player if he gets, say, five times his money. My attitude is that you can't beat honesty and that's where certain people like Ambrose Mendy have let the profession down. George Graham wasn't the first to get caught taking back-handers, and he won't be the last – it's rife. This strong culture of ripping players off has made us more cautious. Silky claims not one player has left him in all his years as an agent but I dispute that.

Tony Finnegan told Walsall what I wanted from them, saying that otherwise I'd sit out my contract. When Colin Lee heard, he said, 'I'll make him come in at seven every morning, including the two weeks off in the summer.' I told Finn, 'No problem, I love training.' Half an hour after he told them my reply, we got what we wanted.

Lee once wanted me to train on a Sunday with the kids after I'd been out the previous night for Vinny Samways' birthday. He left a voicemail message: 'Get your arse in here!' I phoned and told him no because I was going on international duty with Jamaica. When I returned there was a message: I was going on loan to Wigan from 19 November in a swap deal for the rest of the season.

Paul Jewell was the Wigan manager and he left a voicemail saying, 'See you tomorrow, Jamie, and make sure you get out of that pub!' It was a cloudy day, but I turned up wearing dark shades. Jewell was amused. He told a local paper: 'I agreed to let another player leave providing we got cover and it was suggested Jamie came in exchange. Jamie turned up for his first day's training at Wigan in sunglasses. I'm not quite sure where he had come from, but there was certainly no sunshine in Wigan!' Jewell was not impressed with my lack of fitness. I was struggling at first, but soon picked up.

In my four Wigan matches we won three, including a 1-0 home win against Bradford. The old sparkle and commitment that Lee had knocked out of me had returned. The consensus was how come Colin Lee was loaning out a player who was evidently worth picking even in a relegation dogfight – my Wigan form was embarrassing him. Wigan was above Walsall in the Championship and questions about his wisdom were being asked. I'd expected to stay at Wigan for the rest of the season but Lee had to swallow his pride and call me back after a month.

Surprise, surprise, this time he played me. But the balance and confidence at Walsall was by now wrong and we were losing repeatedly, highlighted by a 6-1 defeat at home to Coventry. Walsall was relegated and Lee got sacked. I still feel that had he shown more faith in me, we could have survived. My drinking had never been a problem in the past – he just wanted someone to blame for his own shortcomings.

When approached to give his side of the Walsall story for this book, Aaron Kerr was very complimentary about me. He said that letting him stay in my house in Wolverhampton for four weeks rent-free was the kindest thing anyone in football had done for him. Not surprisingly, there was no mention of informing on me.

The reason why Jimmy Walker got the 'Donny Brasco' nickname was because, like the Mafia film, he vouched for Kerr. Being keepers, they both trained and socialised together. Jimmy convinced me Kerr wouldn't run stories to the gaffer. But you were very, very wrong, Fat Boy – Kerr blew us up.

At Walsall I really got on well with the club doctor, Ralph Rogers. He's still there now. A black American, born in the Bronx who grew up in Northern Jersey, Rogers has been working in sports medicine for twenty years. We bonded straight away. Even though it was Colin Lee who appointed him and they are still friends today, Dr Rogers feels it was a tragedy that I left. 'It was known in the football locker room you were hanging out,' he said to me. 'Liking Guinness is not a crime, damn everybody knows how much you pride yourself on your fitness and physique. Guinness is good for the body – all that iron, you're a testament to that. Anyway, there were other players hanging out. One in particular was really bad, but he didn't get punished – you did.'

Dr Rogers couldn't be too open due to conflict of interests. The day we really bonded was when I went for treatment and told him about my past: 'When you told me about your apprenticeship and how you'd never played for a proper team before prison, I thought, "Damn! This ain't a story, it's a movie."' Rogers says he's never seen me lose my temper because I don't need to – people soon get the message when I say something quietly to them. He was amused when I said, 'If so-and-so is messing with you, don't worry, Doc, I'll take care of it.' When it comes to helping someone I love and respect, there's nothing I'm not prepared to do.

I've got a world of respect for Dr Rogers. A week after he accepted the job from Colin Lee on a handshake, he was offered a position at West Bromwich Albion for three times the money. Being a man of integrity, he declined and has never regretted it. Now that's class. Rogers was told by a West Brom official, 'There's no friendship in football.' A sad statement, but not entirely true.

I scored in my last game for Walsall, at Nottingham Forest, before joining Nicky Law, my former Bradford boss, at Grimsby. Scored on my debut too, in a 4-4 away draw at Chesterfield.

Law made me captain straight away. He wanted a general, and got one. After the murders at Walsall, it was nice to be appreciated again. Law had seen on Sky Sports that I was available and phoned from Grimsby. I agreed straight away – I had to go where the money was, so didn't need to discuss this with Rowena, because she has less choice than me. On my way there, Huddersfield's manager Terry Yorath rang, offering more money and an extra year on the contract. It would have suited me, Huddersfield being still in Yorkshire, but I told him I had already committed to Law. You could say I wanted to stay on the right side of the Law. So much for my bad boy image, but it was nice to be in demand.

We beat Sheffield Wednesday at home, lost at QPR, then needed to win the last two to stay up. When we beat Brentford at home 1-0, it was down to the final game at Tranmere. After a brave fight we lost 2-1 and were sent down. I got a bad knee injury in that match which cost them big-time. Had I been fully fit, I'm sure we would have won. It required nine stitches and was caused by an over-the-top tackle, but I still considered it an accident. The flesh was ripped off and you could see the bare bone of the knee cap. Every time I bent it the stitches came out. But I was only out for a couple of weeks. Law got sacked and my permanent move was gone.

Grimsby deliberately made a poor offer so that it was totally unacceptable for me to live up there. Even though they had gone down a division and had to cut the wages bill, it was rubbish – being captain and a reliable player did not seem to count. My agent Tony Finnegan suggested I try to rejoin Paul Jewell at Wigan. I did well, but busted my hand outside The Puzzle in Battersea. This idiot, Danny Rodmell, told me three times that when we were kids I had pulled his hair and he was still holding a grudge. He tried to butt me. I punched him up and was smashing him so much that he pleaded for mercy.

I landed up in Chelsea and Westminster hospital with a broken arm. It became infected right down to the tendon, probably from his dirty mouth when I smashed his teeth in. Although it wasn't painful at first, it got worse. They washed it out and left it open to heal with some gel, but it didn't work: the tendon got stuck to the skin. Without any anaesthetic, I had to watch whilst they pulled the tendon away, then stitched it up. Luckily, I am a quick healer and within two-and-a-half weeks I was back in training. This was the first time I met two of the Jamaican coaches of that period, Lazaroni and Carl Brown, who came to the Beaufoy Arms. Simon Osbourne point-blank refuses to believe I played for Jamaica. 'I swear you've got a twin of the same name who's impersonating you,' he says. I keep promising him a Jamaica shirt for his little boy and always tell him it's in the post!

Lazaroni is the best coach I've ever worked with. The Brazilian knows football inside out and how to get the best out of players. For example, at training camp he noticed that the Jamaican-based players were not that tight with the England-based players. After a while he figured out what was wrong and called a meeting to clear the air. He got everyone to chat their chat and express themselves. It worked a treat and we bonded beautifully after that. Another time he took me off at half-time. It was Panama away, a World Cup qualifier in October 2004, and we were losing 1-0. Lazaroni said I wasn't doing my job which I resented. Nobody likes to be substituted at half-time, but we drew 1-1 in the end so maybe he was right. He had the bollocks to do it, the courage of his convictions. If I meet him in the future we will sit down and have a proper buzz. He coached Ronaldinho as a kid so you have to respect him to the max.

Once we were playing pool and Lazaroni asked how come I was so good. Prison, I replied. He started laughing and joked about it. He's a real man's man and I respect him deeply.

So at the end of the 2004 season, released by Grimsby, I had no club to go to. After years in the North it was time to go back home. Some of my bredrens from earlier days were now lost to drugs, dead or in prison, including Donny, who's now on the gear. Looking back, I feel he was a leech – and just used me as a meal ticket.

After all the time up and down Britain's motorways I could have made a living as a tour guide to the service stations of Great Britian. My mind was clear; to keep my sanity and maintain a strong relationship with Rowena and my kids I had to return to London. But where?

Chapter 20

ANGRY BEE

For the 2004–5 season I went to Brentford. It was good to be back in London, even though I was paid nothing for the first two games. Andy Myers and Isaiah Rankin were there and they recommended me to manager Martin Allen. Initially I joined on a non-contract basis: the money was nothing like my Bradford days. My previous years in football were good financially, which is why I bought a house in London five years ago. Luckily, when I returned to London, I'd rented out my house in Leeds and put some dough aside.

Good job I planned ahead because it seems that I have a certain bad reputation now when it didn't seem to damage my prospects in the years before. Paul Jewell said if a club wants you then I'll give you a recommendation. But no firm offers came in. Today I train and play with youths and they say, 'Rah, we never knew you could play so good.' I haven't lost anything and still feel capable at thirty-six of playing in the Premiership.

One of the matches I most remember was when we played Bradford at home on 20 November 2004. It was good to see some of my old team-mates. Andy Myers knew I didn't like Dean Windass. To make matters worse, we'd lost 2-1 so I was fuming. Myers tapped him on the shoulder and the geezer turns round, thinking it was me wanting to shake his hand. Myers done it quality and popped to the back of the crowd. 'Alright Jamie?' asked Windass. It was all I could do to hail him back. Myers creased up – he's still laughing to this day.

They were another great bunch at Brentford. Alex Rhodes, a young striker, was the butt of most of our jokes 'cos he was so dim, which is why we called him 'Trigger' after the *Only Fools & Horses* character. When we had to go to Lilleshall together by train, I said to meet at Euston station. Lilleshall is about two hours outside London. Trigger asked, 'Are we going on the underground?' I replied, 'Yeah, District Line all the way.' He believed me!

Martin Allen is praised as a young, talented manager. He was loving me when I first arrived at Brentford and playing me at right-back. I played well, proved myself in the side but when I got injured with a bad knee in January 2005 there seemed to be a conspiracy not to get me fit. Brentford's form was good: we were challenging for a play-off place in League One and I wanted to be part of it all. Damian Doyle, the physio, didn't seem interested in helping me and that's when I demanded to go to Lilleshall. I had to be really assertive and felt there were personal reasons why they were not anxious to get me fit again. People say Allen's going far in management, but if he has ambitions of bigger clubs and players he'll have to learn how to treat them with a bit more respect and understanding. His attitude is if you don't get into line, he'll get rid of you. No wonder his nickname is 'The Animal'. Deon Burton and Andy Myers were experienced pros, too, but he treated us like kids. We'd all played in the Prem and had plenty still to offer the club, but at the end of the season he let us go. But his No.2, Adrian Whitbread, is quality and so too is Johnny Griffiths, the Chief Scout. It wasn't a bad attitude on my part either. I didn't find it hard to get up for a Brentford match – I can get up for a pub team. Not being picked for the play-offs that May (which Brentford lost to Sheffield Wednesday) confirmed what was clear: there was no future for me at Griffin Park.

Allen called me in and said I was a diamond geezer, but he didn't have a place in the club for me anymore. He warned me that when I've had a drink, I go a bit dark. 'I don't want to see you go back to jail, Jamie,' he said. Very tactful, eh? 'Be careful, when you've had a drink, you're dangerous.' I think that stems from the time the previous Christmas when the physio (who was only about twenty-five) was always trying to embarrass a South Korean kid, who lived in east London and didn't know his way around. Whenever he came in late on public transport, Damian told him off in front of us. At the Christmas party Damian said something I didn't like. I told him, 'I'm not Sam Lee 'cos I will kill you.' He must have told Allen and I assume that's what he meant. In my opinion, all he's good for is lifting weights – that seems to be his cure for everything!

Allen and I had our differences, but we tolerated each other – I even made him laugh without trying. At the end of the 2005 season club dinner at a hotel in Heathrow, everyone wore tuxedos. I had the whole nine yards, but forgot to bring my shoes; ended up wearing my grey trainers. Allen said, 'Only Jamie Lawrence could turn up in a tux wearing his trainers.'

Before things went off-key, Allen even adopted a piece of my music for the big games we would play on the bus. He knew about my past, but also understood that I had a close-knit family and that was the most important thing to me. Allen said that I always conducted myself the right way: no sulking or moodiness. That meeting at the end of the season wasn't easy, but at least he was honest: he had to plan for the future and wanted to bring in some new players. He thanked me and even invited me back to pre-season training, if I wanted, and said not to call him 'gaffer' anymore but 'Martin' instead because I was now a friend and he was not my boss. He wanted to be friends forever, which sounded pretty nice, considering I'd only known him a while.

But Allen's sentiments were insincere. For example, he asked how I'd survived at Brentford on only £500 a week before tax. 'With great difficulty,' I replied. Taking home just over £300 does not give a family man with a mortgage any great quality of life. Good job I'd put some aside. Allen had the cheek to ask me, even though he was the one who put me on that school-leavers' money. He had his much better paid favourites. The only reason I'd stayed was I had to be at a club to play for Jamaica in the World Cup qualifiers. Life is full of ironies. If I hadn't busted my hand smashing Danny Rodmell, I could have joined Paul Jewell's Wigan on a week-to-week basis on much better 'paper'. I really only started at Brentford to get fit. By the time I got match fit, I injured my knee, which kept me out for a while.

Even though I'm thankful for the opportunity, the way man treated man was bare disrespect – I'm not feeling it. Allen is one of those characters who would like to rule everything! He claims he has every confidence in me becoming a good manager, partly because I've had some difficult life experiences, but also because he feels I'm a good people person; he advised me to get my coaching badges and maybe start at non-league level. He said time will tell and I'm a natural leader.

Nice glowing tributes, but after all that word was coming back to me that he was bad-mouthing me to people in football who were asking if I was worth a chance. A couple of Championship teams were interested, but when Allen dissed me they didn't want to know. I was meant to go to Watford to train, but because they heard certain things about me, they pulled the plug on it. Allen needs to control his emotions a little better – he sometimes got so mad he would attack the blackboard, punching it up.

Another Brentford man I didn't like was John Salako. He played for England a couple of times, but lost some pace after injury and was never picked again. Salako thinks he's a Big-Time Charlie and just because he gets TV work, he's better than most. Both him and his missus said to Rowena when they saw her at the Christmas party that they didn't think she would be that attractive. They told her they thought she'd be a bimbo, too. Bang out of order! I put it to Salako and he was shitting himself, couldn't even talk. He stayed far from me after that. Born in Nigeria, he's half-African, yet he don't acknowledge any of his black side. Once he even made some snide comment about not letting black people in his house. Just for fun in training we sometimes played black v white, but when it came to Salako we said we didn't want him...

* * * * *

I'm a player-fitness coach at non-league Fisher Athletic in south London now and I'm enjoying it, although I still feel capable of playing at a higher level. Fisher have a lot of talented players and a good, ambitious chairman. Top man! They're in the Rymans Premier League and have ambitions of getting into the Football League. At Fisher Athletic, I've noticed the lower you come down the football ladder, the more big-time the players think they are. No matter what their ability, they all think they're Pelé. When one banter got really heavy I said to someone, 'You know what, when you get two days to spare, I'll take you round my wardrobe.' That shut him up. I showed some Fisher lads the pictures of me with the Brazilian players and one was so impressed, he said, 'I ain't gonna give you no more banter again.'

I know their assistant coach, Warren Hackett, from my Bradford days. He's quality. Players I train include Ben Walshe, Anthony Rivière, Leroy Griffiths and Mad Dog – a good bunch. In the short time I've been there, I've really bonded with two players in particular: Walshie and Rivs. They've got no airs and graces, we're proper close. People even know us as 'Three Green Bottles' (when one doesn't come out, we sing 'Two Green Bottles').

Mentoring is something I'd like to do on a big scale. I already do it on an informal basis and one of my little prodigies is Ryan McKenzie, a twenty-one-year-old student from Lavender Hill. He openly admits he was involved in bad things and with a quick temper he could have ended up killing a man and doing twenty-five years bird. By talking to him calmly and encouraging him to steer clear of bad influences, he has gone down the right path. Another one is my cousin Adrian Ward. I got him a trial at Bradford and he lived with me for a couple of months to get away from the bad influences in London.

The things I saw as a kid, it's a wonder I wasn't traumatised. At fourteen I saw the blood in the corridor from an older kid who had been messing with a gun and accidentally shot himself dead in the head. If I can save at least one person from doing that or witnessing that kind of thing, I'll be satisfied.

My bredrens have always been very special to me, so when they get into trouble I will help them to the hilt. One time we were in a jeweller's in Hatton Garden, central London. Fat Sam had picked me up from King's Cross train station. I saw something I liked in a jeweller's and decided to go back to Bradford then come back the next day. Madness, doing all that travelling, but I had my reasons. I had red hair at the time, everyone knew who I was with my red hair. The next day, the same jeweller, Alex, says to Fat Sam: 'You're Ben, aren't you?' Alex deliberately kept us talking for about fifteen minutes. A menacing man in a long coat came in and looked at Fat Sam. It was obvious he was intending to do something because he reached for something in his coat but realised he wasn't the right man. Alex was rumbled: Ben put it on them. Alex comes like a puss now when I see him. My saying is, 'long chase, short catch.' It's alright being a bad boy in a crowd, but sometimes you're not in a crowd.

Someone who doesn't need a crowd is my bredren Gee, my bona fide. I know you're going through some difficult times at the moment but just remember I've got bare love for you and I appreciate everything you have done for me. When I needed a friend you were there. Big up your status. There is only one like you. To Fat Sam, words can't put into context what you mean to me. You have always been there for me and my family and you're more like a brother than a friend. You don't see me as a 'baller, you see me as me. Your heart is clean and I love you and your mum. And to Big Nose Speller. You have been there and seen everything. You know I've got mad love for you. You're like my arms and legs. You have been everywhere with me, good and bad and it's like you're like my white Siamese twin.

It's been an eventful journey so far. At least I can safely say my life up to this point has not been boring. It effectively started with that slash across Donovan's neck over the snooker bet and took me along the craziest rollercoaster ride in football history.

After all the hectic years of travelling, endless hotel rooms and irregular hours, it's nice to be working regular hours and still be involved in football. For the time being I'm happy to be there for all my kids. Nathan is an absolute diamond but round his mum's he can be bad. It's because I'm not there 24-7. Being up north for much of my career I didn't have much time for him. I'd love to dedicate the next few years to seeing him and Tiagh grow up. Nathan is a good little footballer and I'm going to nurture his talent. With Tiagh, I couldn't ask for a better kid. It's like getting a second chance to be a father again. When I have bad days, a hug from her just makes my troubles go away. I love both of them with all my heart. Both kids are credits to their mothers.

What I want to do now is help all those kids out there with talent, to work with them and steer them away from crime. There is a legal way to earn good money. I'm living proof. There are bredrens out there doing bad things. Badness is not the way. It's harder to go out there and do a trade for a couple of years and work your way up. But kids have to learn to stick to it. I want to visit youth offenders' institutions and talk to them. I'm not one to go on stage and make speeches but I like doing a proper one-to-one. They must understand that if you do something bad to a brudda then there is a knock-on effect. If you kill someone you know it's serious from there and you'll have to move in different ways just to stay alive. I wish I'd had good people around me when I was their age. Some just need guidance. If they get a bigger man's perspective who has been down the bad route then they will listen. I can do that. I'm at the crossroads of my life now after twelve years as a pro. It's hard not being involved. Players don't look forward to pre-season training. I loved it. Not just the physical side, it was a time to catch up with your bredrens after the summer holidays.

I want to big up all my family, especially Elfreda. As my tattoo says: 'Mum is everything to me. Love you with all my heart. Thanks for all the years devoted to me. Your loving son James Lawrence.' My sister Val has been there at crucial times of need. Solid as a rock. She's ragga too. Tell you what time of day it is.

In the future I don't want major dough, just want to be able to give something back. Youths think there's only one way out, but I've seen too many of my people – white as well as black – go the wrong way. I hope this book inspires at least one kid to do something positive with his or her talent.

Playing in the Premiership again is now just a pipe dream. But I'm going to get my coaching badges and strongly believe I can work at the top level again, either as a coach or manager. James Lawrence has gone from prison to the Premiership once and I'm sure I can do it again.